EXPLORING
FAITH
Theology for Life

SERIES EDITORS: Leslie J Francis and Jeff Astley

BEING ANGLICAN

Alastair Redfern

D0452997

DARTON·LONGMAN+TODD

First published in 2000 by
Darton, Longman and Todd Ltd
1 Spencer Court
140-142 Wandsworth High Street
London SW18 4JJ

ISBN 0-232-52369-X

A catalogue record for this book is available from the British Library.

Designed by Sandie Boccacci
Phototypeset in Minion by Intype London Ltd
Printed and bound in Great Britain by
Page Bros, Norwich, Norfolk

CONTENTS

ACKNOWLEDGEMENTS

Quotations from the Bible are from the *Good News Bible* unless otherwise indicated.

PREFACE

At the beginning of the third millennium a new mood is sweeping through the Christian Churches. This mood is reflected in a more radical commitment to discipleship among a laity who wish to be theologically informed and fully equipped for Christian ministry in the secular world.

Exploring Faith: theology for life is designed for people who want to take Christian theology seriously. Taken seriously, Christian theology engages the mind, involves the heart, and seeks active expression in the way we live. Those who explore their faith in this way are beginning to shape a theology for life.

Exploring Faith: theology for life is rooted in the individual experience of the world and in the ways through which God is made known in the world. Such experience is related to and interpreted in the light of the Christian tradition. Each volume in the series takes a key aspect of theology, and explores this aspect in dialogue with the readers' own experience. Each volume is written by a scholar who has clear authority in the area of theology discussed and who takes seriously the ways in which busy adults learn.

The volumes are suitable for all those who wish to learn more about the Christian faith and ministry, including those who have already taken Christian basic courses (such as *Alpha* and *Emmaus*) and have been inspired to undertake further study, those preparing to take theology as an undergraduate course, and those already engaged on degree programmes. The volumes have been developed for individuals to work on alone or for groups to study together.

Already groups of Christians are using the *Exploring Faith: theology for life* series throughout the United Kingdom, linked by an exciting initiative pioneered jointly by the Anglican dioceses, the Board of Education of the Church and World Division and the Ministry Division of the Archbishops' Council of the Church of England, the National

Society and the Church Colleges. Used in this way each volume can earn credits towards one of the Church Colleges' Certificates and provide access to degree level study. Further information about the Church Colleges' Certificate Programme is provided on page 141.

The Church Colleges' Certificate Programme integrates well with the lifelong learning agenda which now plays such a crucial role in educational priorities. Learning Christians can find their way into degree-bearing programmes through this series *Exploring Faith: theology for life* linked with the Church Colleges' Certificates.

This series of books originated in materials developed by and for the Aston Training Scheme. Thanks are due to former staff of the Scheme, and in particular to Roger Spiller who conceived of and commissioned the original series, and to Nicola Slee who edited the original materials. In the light of the closure of Aston, this series represents something of the ongoing contribution of the Scheme to the life of the Church.

In preparing a series of this kind, much work is done behind the scenes. Financial and staff support have been generously given by the Ministry Division. Thanks are due to Marilyn Parry for the vision of bringing together the Aston materials and the Anglican Church Colleges of Higher Education. We are also grateful for financial support from the following Church Colleges: Chester College; Christchurch University College, Canterbury; The College of St Mark & St John, Plymouth; St Martin's College, Lancaster; Trinity College Carmarthen; and Whitelands College (Roehampton Institute). Without the industry, patience, perception, commitment and skill of Ruth Ackroyd this series would have remained but a dream.

The series editors wish to express their personal thanks to colleagues who have helped them shape the series identity, especially Diane Drayson, Evelyn Jackson and Katie Worrall, and to the individual authors who have produced high quality text on schedule and so generously accepted firm editorial direction. The editorial work has been supported by the North of England Institute for Christian Education and the Centre for Ministry Studies at the University of Wales, Bangor.

Leslie J Francis
Jeff Astley

INTRODUCTION

Anglicanism exists in the eye of the believer. Much of the teaching of Jesus is a call and a challenge to people to learn:
- to see – conversion is being able to say 'I was blind, and now I can see' (John 9:25);
- and to believe – 'Your faith has saved you' (Matthew 9:22).

The Anglican tradition takes seriously that learning to see is an ongoing, dynamic process and that believing needs a focus and a framework to allow such growth and development.

There is no clearly defined exclusive Anglican theology: rather the Church of England, more self-consciously since the Reformation, has pioneered a way of being part of the one, holy, catholic and apostolic Church, which is appropriate to its particular context, open to new possibilities and also contributes to the fruitfulness of the universal Church.

This book invites you to explore and test some of the key features of the Anglican tradition as it has developed, initially in Britain and more recently across the world. There is a particular emphasis upon the value of Anglicanism as a resource for ecumenism and for presenting the Gospel in a plural world.

The format of the book enacts something fundamental about 'being Anglican' in that it depends upon the active participation of the reader: Anglicanism exists in the eye of the believer.

The first chapter explores the issue of being Anglican and examines theories of unity in such a diverse Church, together with the debate about appropriate marks of distinctiveness.

Subsequent chapters offer an overview of the development of Anglican theology and spirituality from the sixteenth century to the present day, using case studies of key figures who represent both the variety and also the rootedness of Anglicanism. This includes an appreciation of the pastoral tradition and its relationship to the parochial system and the notion of a national Church, together with an insight into the foundations of Anglican spirituality. Further topics explore the approach to mission in an indifferent and pluralistic world; styles of ministry and organisation; the tradition of prophecy and political involvement (public witness and social concern); developing models for valuing the inclusivism of the parish and the distinctiveness of the Gospel; and the worldwide spread of the Anglican tradition.

This book does not offer a comprehensive history but rather a series of snapshots of people and of principles. You are invited to engage here with a moving, living target.

I have avoided detailed discussion of the classical 'parties' of evangelical, catholic and liberal, partly because this analysis oversimplifies the nature of Anglicanism and partly because it is in the continuing interplay between the various manifestations of the Anglican tradition and their respective contexts that this particular way of making Church thrives.

The Anglican tradition does not bear too much detailed scrutiny; that is not its purpose. Rather it has grown and developed as a way of inviting those engaged in the human struggle to see and believe, and to participate in the resources, rhythms and resonances of the catholic Church in a manner which is appropriate to local conditions and challenges.

Anglicanism exists in the eye of the believer; it will be enriched by all who contribute to it with commitment and vigour.

1. BEING ANGLICAN

Introduction

The basic text for exploring the Anglican tradition is found in the second collect for 'The Order for Evening Prayer' in *The Book of Common Prayer*: 'O God, From whom all holy desires, all good counsels, and all just works do proceed: Give unto thy servants that peace which the world cannot give.'

This prayer has an ancient pedigree and connects with European catholic Christianity. It also claims a radical inclusivity – all good thoughts and actions are to do with God, whether or not people recognise this fact. Thus harmony and wholeness for all human endeavour come as gifts from God.

This foundation, expressed in liturgy, provides no discernible focus such as a papal ruler or a written basis of faith. Rather, there is a way of being Anglican that springs from the participation in the worship and witness of the Church by all kinds of people, in all kinds of situations. There is a radical inclusivism, dependent upon and conjoined in the gift of God's grace; human structures and formulae are secondary and supportive. Anglicanism is a living, changing phenomenon which operates by involving and embracing a large range of people and experiences. This first chapter explores this notion of 'being Anglican'.

Reflecting on experience

Think of three contrasting experiences you have had of being on a journey. Highlight what is common to these experiences and what is different or unique about each one. Give some thought to the significance of place and geography, other people, your own hopes and fears, and the process of travelling.

EXERCISE

📖 **Read Acts 1.** Drawing on your experiences of journeying, consider:
- the instruction not to leave Jerusalem, but 'to wait for the gift my Father promised' (v. 4);
- that apostles must be those who have travelled the journey 'from the time John preached his message of baptism until the day Jesus was taken up from us to heaven' (vv. 21– 22);
- 'you will be witnesses . . . to the ends of the earth' (v. 8).

Seeing and believing

Being Anglican represents a commitment to honour and live with a range of approaches and experiences, taking seriously the specific context of people but requiring this to be put against the story of Jesus from his birth in Bethlehem to his ascension into heaven.

In Anglicanism, there has never been an attempt to systematise Christian experience into a single set of views or practices. Thus there are few boundaries; the focus is on what is common – the desire to share something together – rather than upon what divides and distinguishes. Systems of authority have been transient and malleable: the characteristically Anglican mechanisms of checks and balances has tended to prevail. More important has been the desire to embrace people in a common sense of worship and in a common culture of Christianity-in-the-community.

Being Anglican

The marks of Anglicanism presented in this section are not intended to be definitive, but rather to indicate some of the key elements in the working of Anglicanism.

Corporate worship and the centrality of Christ

Being Anglican is rooted in the discipline of corporate worship, focused in *The Book of Common Prayer*. In recent times, the advent of *The Alternative Service Book 1980*, and many equivalents worldwide, has been on the presumption of a basic commitment to common prayer and corporate worship. It is this that provides the bedrock and testing ground for human life. It offers a framework and guide both for individual experience of God and for personal devotion. The notion of common prayer also allows great latitude in terms of local usage.

This 'mark' of being Anglican is grounded in Richard Hooker's doctrine of participation (see Chapter 2). God calls us to know him more clearly by participating in his life and in his love, which involves participating in the life and love of others who are also created and called by God. Hence there is an essential corporateness to the experience of God's grace, which is best focused in common worship.

A nineteenth-century Anglican teacher, F D Maurice, put this starkly: 'The spirit in an individual is a fearful contradiction' (Maurice, 1885, p. 209). To be one with the Spirit of God is to be one not only with God, but with all others in whom the Holy Spirit lives. It is impossible to be an individual as a Christian. The Holy Spirit makes us one with God and one with all of God's creatures. Worship is rooted in the corporate. Moreover, for Hooker as for Maurice, the key to Christian corporation is the person of Christ. Christians are one in the body of Christ. Jesus is the one who embraces all and includes all. The Spirit calls us to be one in him.

The Book of Common Prayer calls us to participation in Christ, focused in common worship.

The incarnation is foundational

The extraordinary and the ordinary exist in a dynamic relationship. The extraordinary love of God is often revealed in very ordinary things, from the baby in Bethlehem to bread and wine in worship. The incarnation shows us God's love and life made flesh in this world. For Anglicans this has meant a strong emphasis upon digging deeper into the ordinariness of human living as a key to receiving more of this extraordinary love of God. This is at the root of the Anglican pastoral tradition.

Human experience is essential: the occasional offices

In contrast to a tendency in much western Christianity, both Reformed and Catholic, to denigrate human experience, the Anglican tradition has been realistic and positive about its importance. Hence a structure is provided for recognising before God the key elements in the human cycle. *The Book of Common Prayer* provides opportunities for everyone in the community to locate and explore the significance of birth, marriage, sickness, confession and death, within the larger context of God's mysterious power and purposes. Formative human experiences are marked and evaluated within the context of corporate worship.

Today there is a move to mark other key human experiences within the much larger context of the hopes and fears which Christians call the Kingdom. For example, 'new occasional offices' have been framed for the blessing of homes, owning failed relationships, the loss of or change in employment, or the launching of new groupings for family life.

The primacy of pastoral practice

Great stress is laid upon God's love experienced as care and goodness in human beings living together – in relationships that are personal, local or wider. The resources of the Church's doctrine and liturgy are servants rather than masters of this reality. The occasional offices provide a framework for pastoral practice and the particular role of the ordained ministry.

The importance of order

Being Anglican is based on the notion of order. Creation works by order emerging from chaos, as the gift of God. Order is essential for Christian believing and thus doctrine provides a vital framework for the individual experience of grace. Similarly, order is important in worship and this is achieved by having common forms and texts. In ministry there is a structure of bishops, priests and deacons who are responsible for the authenticity of word and sacrament. In fact all human living requires order, and the Church therefore offers a sequence of offices to mark and monitor key moments.

However, this kind of order and structure is not infallible. Article 21 of the Thirty-Nine Articles of Religion says that councils can and do err. Archbishop Laud (see Chapter 4) was clear that bishops can make mistakes that may need to be corrected by a college of bishops. Hooker recognised that the structures for Church life may need to change.

Anglican tradition recognises that order is essential but that its particular forms may change.

A parochial not a gathered Church

Being Anglican involves a commitment to welcome and include all who live in each parish. Every resident is seen as a potential member of the Anglican Church if they choose to take up this invitation, hence the right to be baptised or married in the church of the parish in which a person resides. This means that the life of the Church is never organised solely for the benefit of those who attend but always with an eye to the needs and potential contributions of everyone else in the community.

This mark of being Anglican is rooted in English religious culture. In the worldwide Anglican Communion, however, Churches are more gathered and confessional.

Ambiguity and provisionality are important

Being Anglican involves exercising a reluctance to push too hard to make boundaries that exclude. *All* good things can contribute to the coming of the Kingdom, even if on the surface they seem to raise contradictions and tensions.

The making of Church, the living of the Christian life, the understanding of the Gospel and the requirement of order – all these things must be 'provisional' in this life. The Anglican tradition has always recognised the variety of ways in which these issues can be explored, and the reality that new things can only be received by those willing to accept change and development.

Loose ends are acceptable

Anglican tradition holds together a wide range of theological stances. It recognises that much learning comes from comparing experiences and exploring differences positively. This approach values intuition as well as logic, faith as well as formulas and process as well as context.

Thus being Anglican involves living with a certain amount of untidiness.

The Lambeth quadrilateral

In 1888 the Lambeth Conference of Anglican Bishops (which meets every ten years) agreed a quadrilateral of 'essentials' for the unity and integrity of the Anglican tradition. The four articles are as follows:

- The Holy Scriptures of the Old and New Testaments, as 'containing all things necessary to salvation', and as being the rule and ultimate standard of faith.
- The Apostles' Creed, as the Baptismal Symbol; and the Nicene Creed, as the sufficient statement of the Christian Faith.
- The two Sacraments ordained by Christ Himself – Baptism and the Supper of the Lord – ministered with unfailing use of Christ's words of Institution, and of the elements ordained by Him.
- The Historic Episcopate, locally adapted in the methods of its administration to the varying needs of the nations and peoples called by God into the Unity of His Church. (Stephenson, 1978, p. 5)

Each of the 'essentials' is open to a wide range of interpretations. Being

Anglican does not emphasise the importance of constructing systems, despite our strong human desire for the security and stability that might appear to be created by such means. Rather, the Anglican concern has been to be open to new factors and possibilities. Thus there is no systematic Anglican theology: just a large variety of theologians, each rooted in a particular context.

However, the quadrilateral lists essentials that are all key components of common worship. Being Anglican is to recognise that it is in worship, and the atmosphere of structured ambiguity that worship provides, that all our penultimate strivings meet the ultimate.

Comprehensiveness
Being Anglican is *not* about the kind of comprehensiveness that brings everything together in a single system. The comprehensiveness of the Anglican tradition tries to witness to the comprehensiveness of God.

EXERCISE

Look again at the ten marks of being Anglican outlined earlier. What is your reaction to them? Is there anything you would question or subtract? Is there anything extra you would add? How do these marks compare with your experience of other Churches?

What are the reasons for your reactions?

Being Anglican with others: some theories of unity

Since the Reformation there have been three major theories for trying to hold together the variety within the Anglican tradition to give a sense of unity as a Church.

Each theory recognises that Anglicanism is not 'confessional', in the sense of having a clearly stated set of doctrines that must be accepted by every member of the Church. Neither is Anglicanism 'experiential', in the sense of being based upon the presupposition that all adherents will have a particular and common experience of God.

The Book of Common Prayer: worship and pragmatism
This theory argues that the diversity of belief and behaviour that constitutes Anglicanism is held together by a discipline of common

worship, with all members participating in the worship of the one God through an agreed set form. The worship may be understood and expressed in a variety of ways but there is a unifying binding element. The common text does not require a single confessional or experiential approach but the discipline of using a set form produces a pragmatic unity.

Historically this has been a powerful unifying force within Anglicanism. However, the advent of alternative service books, a shift from set text to alternatives and the notion of a common 'structure' for worship has seriously weakened its effectiveness.

Theological method

The second theory of unity for Anglicanism has been a commitment to a distinctive method of doing theology, based upon the dynamic of Scripture, tradition and reason.

The interplay of these elements produces variety, not least because Scripture can be interpreted in a number of ways, tradition accumulates and thereby changes, and reason tends to accentuate differences as much as produce harmony. Nonetheless, the commitment to an interaction of these elements has been seen as the bedrock of an open but unifying method in theology.

In practice, much Anglican theology has shown little appreciation of tradition (apart from the Fathers and the Caroline divines) and the relationship between those who wish to give priority to Scripture (sometimes labelled 'evangelicals') or to reason ('liberals') or to tradition ('catholics') has been one of tension between rival and competing systems, rather than a recognition of an integrative method offering a common focus.

Episcopacy

The third focus of Anglican identity and unity has been episcopacy: bishops as appointed leaders. This theory presupposes a wide variety of belief and behaviour among clergy and laity who all own a common obedience and relationship to the bishop. This is formally recognised in confirmation and ordination vows, and in the licensing of clergy to particular posts.

This model applies also to the parish system, where the incumbent is the local 'episcope' who provides a focus for unity in the Church and for the wider community. The parson has a duty to be minister to all the people in a parish if they choose to claim such service.

Once again, this theory has been found wanting in times of dispute and tension within the Church. The system of freehold provides clergy with a powerful independence from the bishop, and the laity increasingly expect oversight to be negotiated and earned in relation to their own particular needs.

EXERCISE

The three theories of Anglican unity are rooted in common worship, theological method and episcopacy. How do these theories relate to your own experience of Christians seeking unity? What are the strengths and weaknesses of each theory?

How might synodical government serve as a structure for holding diversity together? Are there other models of uniting Christians in a common enterprise (for example Christian Aid unites different Churches in social action)?

Do you have any further thoughts about the proper relationship between local context and a common story and journey?

Fundamentalism: the key to unity

Fundamentalism has become increasingly important in the world of massive change and turbulence that was ushered in by the industrial revolution. An example is the cult of the Holy Father in nineteenth-century Roman Catholicism, which gave people something secure and certain in a time of confusion and instability: an infallible Pope who could be trusted to know and to provide protective guidance and direction. This fundamentalism was pastorally and spiritually effective.

Fundamentalism has a long pedigree! There is something in human beings which requires security, stability and shelter; religious systems often meet this need in direct proportion to their own clarity and certainty.

The Anglican tradition is steeped in a number of fundamentalisms: about Scripture, about tradition, about the human ability to think. But whereas most people see a fundamentalism as an all-embracing system for themselves, to the exclusion of others, in Anglicanism there has always been room for people to be deeply committed and fundamentalist about their own particular approach, while paradoxically subscribing to the fact that they will be in dialogue (if only implicitly) with others who are different, through being locked in a common system of worship or a common way of doing theology or a common focus of unity and obedience.

However fundamentalist Anglicans have been, their Anglicanism is a sign of accepting their part in a larger scenario, even if their own identity and nourishment comes from something much narrower and includes a desire to change others accordingly. In this sense a working definition for the variety-in-unity of the Anglican tradition might be: *Anglicanism is about fundamentalisms in dialogue.* This recognises the importance of particular contexts and approaches (staying in Jerusalem, Acts 1:4) and also the possibility of other places and perspectives (travelling the journey, Acts 1:21–22).

One of the enduring strengths of being Anglican is the ability to recognise the need of many people to be fundamentalist (even about liberalism!) in respect of the particular approach that gives them nourishment and focus, while allowing them to be part of a structure that can facilitate dialogue, co-existence and common worship with others of very different persuasions.

EXERCISE

'Anglicanism is about fundamentalisms in dialogue.' How do you react to this notion? What is the difference between fundamentalism and prejudice? How may the two be separated?

Being Anglican: the title deeds

It is not uncommon to suppose that the Church of England came into existence in the sixteenth century. In fact, the Church of England claims an unbroken and direct connection with the early Church.

The first Anglican apologists recognised that when the Church was initially established there was a tension between Jesus directing that the Gospel be preached to all nations (so the Gospel is universal) and the fact that on the day of Pentecost each heard the Gospel in his or her own language (so the Gospel is always localised). This is the tension which Anglicans claim is of the essence of how God works in the world, and central to the spread of the Gospel in Britain.

Thus when the Christian faith first developed in these islands, what is now called Celtic Christianity became a distinctive and unique branch of the Church, rooted in British culture. It was part of the universal

Church and yet had its own local ways of operating. Similarly, when Pope Gregory sent Augustine from Rome in 597 to establish the Church, the leader of the one, holy, catholic and apostolic Church wrote:

> My brother, you are familiar with the usage of the Roman church in which you were brought up. But if you find customs, whether in the church of Rome or of Gaul or of any other that may be more acceptable to God, I wish you to make a careful selection of them and teach the Church of the English whatever you have been able to learn with profit from various churches. Teach from the various churches what will make sense and help them. For things should not be loved for the sake of places but places for the sake of good things. Choose therefore from every church those things that are pious, religious and upright. And when you have, as it were, made them up into one body, let the minds of the English become accustomed thereunto. (Marshall, 1984, p. 43)

The Pope also wrote:

> It will be impossible to eradicate all errors at one stroke. Just as the man who sets out to climb a high mountain does not advance by leaps and bounds but goes step by step and pace by pace. This is the way the Lord revealed himself to the Israelite people. And since we hold the same faith, that is why customs vary in different churches. (Marshall, 1984, p. 43)

We find expressed here the title deeds of how being Anglican has been understood. When missionaries were sent from Rome the Pope recognised, and commissioned Augustine to allow, variety: to choose and use from different places what would connect the Gospel with English culture. The universal Church needs a local flavour.

This is what the Church of England has always valued. At the Reformation it claimed its right to maintain a local flavour over against the centralising authority of the Roman Catholic Church. In the sixteenth century the Church of England called upon the Roman Church to reform itself in certain ways but also to recognise that it was acceptable to be part of the Catholic Church in an English way. There needs to be dialogue between a universal Gospel and the fact that people grow and develop in different ways in different places. This Pentecost principle is one that the Roman Catholic Church has begun to rediscover since the Second Vatican Council.

These title deeds have defined being Anglican since the earliest days of Christianity in Britain. Their continuity can be marked by statements from the Lambeth Conference of 1968:

> Comprehensiveness is an attitude of mind which Anglicans have learned from the thought-provoking controversies of their history ... comprehensiveness demands agreement on fundamentals, while tolerating disagreement on matters in which Christians may differ without feeling the necessity of breaking communion. In the mind of an Anglican comprehensiveness is not about compromise. . . . Rather it implies that the apprehension of truth is a growing thing. . . . It has been the tradition of Anglicanism to contain within one body both Protestant and Catholic elements. But there is a continuing search for the whole truth in which these elements will find complete reconciliation. Comprehensiveness implies a certain slowness . . . we believe that in leading us into the truth the Holy Spirit may have some surprises in store for us in the future as it has had in the past. (Lambeth Conference, 1968, pp. 140–141)

In these words of bishops coming together from Anglicanism all over the world there is a concern to recognise a process that will have surprises in it and will be about change, a process that will be about gradualness and will recognise that different areas are at different stages in different ways. Truth and maturity come through discovery, dialogue and conflict, focused in a commitment to a greater commonness in the body of Christ. This represents the highest ideals of being Anglican.

EXERCISE

Pope Gregory wrote, 'Teach the Church of the English whatever you have been able to learn with profit from the various churches. Teach from the various churches what will make sense and help them.' What might be the criteria for deciding what can be best learned from the various churches?

The Lambeth Conference in 1968 stated, 'The apprehension of truth is a growing thing . . . a continuing search for the whole truth . . . comprehensiveness implies a certain slowness . . . we believe that in leading us into the truth the Holy Spirit may have some surprises in store for us in the future as it has had in the past.' How do you evaluate such sentiments? Who should judge the pace at which to proceed? ▶▶

'Truth and maturity come through discovery, dialogue and con-flict, focused in a commitment to a greater commonness in the body of Christ.' Can you think of ways in which conflict can be handled creatively?

How do your initial reflections about journeying relate to this theme of unity in variety?

EXERCISE

📖 **Read Acts 2:1–12.** How might this passage illuminate or cri-tique this introduction to being Anglican? You may consider:

- the importance of a common place;
- the gift of grace that comes from outside, from beyond this particular context, yet into its midst;
- that each participant was given a new language, an ability to connect with the words and cultures of those who were dif-ferent from themselves;
- that there is one Spirit, who unites all this vibrant diversity;
- that the outcome of this initial experience is a question: 'What does this mean?'
- that there is a need for interpretation to deepen connection and participation.

Further reading

Avis, P (1989), *Anglicanism and the Christian Church*, Edinburgh, T and T Clark.

Bunting, I (ed.) (1996), *Celebrating the Anglican Way*, London, Hodder and Stoughton.

Dickens, A G (1989), *The English Reformation*, London, Batsford (second edition).

Edwards, D (1989), *Christian England*, London, Collins.

McAdoo, H R (1991), *Anglican Heritage: theology and spirituality*, Norwich, Can-terbury Press.

Marshall, M (1984), *The Anglican Church Today and Tomorrow*, Oxford, Mowbray.

Neill, S (1958), *Anglicanism*, Harmondsworth, Penguin.

Stephenson, A M G (1978), *Anglicanism and the Lambeth Conferences*, London, SPCK.

Sykes, S W (1978), *The Integrity of Anglicanism*, Oxford, Mowbray.

Sykes, S and Booty, J (eds) (1988), *The Study of Anglicanism*, London, SPCK.

Wand, J W C (1961), *Anglicanism in History and Today*, London, Weidenfeld and Nicolson.

2. FOUNDATION AND FRAMEWORK

Introduction

The person who is generally credited with providing a foundation and a framework for the Anglican Church is Richard Hooker. Key elements in Hooker's teaching are the doctrine of participation and the bringing together of the ordinary and the extraordinary. This chapter will examine his legacy and invite you to consider its significance for today.

Reflecting on experience

Think of an example of a dispute or conflict between an individual and their family or peer group.

- What should be the rights and duties of the individual?
- What should be the rights and duties of the family or peer group?
- Who can adjudicate between them, and on what grounds?

EXERCISE

📖 **Read Acts 2:12–21.** Consider the competing claims of:
- those who were amazed and confused and kept asking each other, 'What does this mean?' (v. 12);
- those who said that the believers were drunk (v. 13);
- fellow Jews and all who lived in Jerusalem.

What can we learn from the quotation from Joel used by Peter?

Richard Hooker (1554–1600)

A biographical sketch will provide significant clues to Hooker's theology. He was born in Exeter, and eventually became a scholar and then a fellow at Corpus Christi College in Oxford. As a young university teacher he went to stay with friends one weekend when he had a heavy cold. The mistress of the house said, 'You need a wife to look after you; I'll find you one.' The intended wife turned out to be this lady's daughter, Joan. Hooker's biographer writes, 'She brought him neither beauty nor portion.' But Hooker married her. The result was that he could no longer be a fellow at Corpus because at that time an Oxford college was much more like a religious community and only single people could be resident tutors. His biographer comments, 'He was drawn from the tranquillity of his college, to the corroding cares which attend a married priest and a country vicarage' (Walton, 1973, p. 178). Hooker had to give up his fellowship and become a married vicar.

There are stories of his friends going to visit the family and finding Hooker trying to read and continue his holy life and scholarship, but being distracted by the need to tend the sheep and by Joan calling him to help with the baby. That is a significant picture: Hooker trying to be the scholar, the saintly, holy person on the classical model, and yet deeply enmeshed in the everyday messiness and ordinariness of living. His theology developed out of these two things coming together. He came to see that the life of God is known by participating in both worlds: in the ordinary and in the set apart, the extraordinary.

Hooker wrote a great work called *Of The Laws of Ecclesiastical Polity* which developed these views. In his writing he was trying to help the Church of England to crystallise an identity that was confident to be over against Rome but also confident to be over against the puritans, the radical Protestants who were especially powerful at that time. For Rome the great appeal was to tradition. For the puritans the great appeal was to Scripture. Hooker tried to value both of those things but he also had a strong notion of the importance of reason, and of the dynamic between Scripture, tradition and reason which is the theme of classical Anglican theology. In accordance with the Thirty-Nine Articles, he was very firm in stressing that Scripture had priority and contains all that is needed for salvation.

Theological foundation: a hierarchy of laws

Hooker was deeply influenced by the thinking of Aristotle and of Aquinas, which undergirded the tradition of medieval theology. Thus he based his ideas upon the notion of law as something that provided an integrated and all-embracing framework for understanding God, the Christ, the world and the Gospel for human beings. He outlined a hierarchy of laws.

- *The law eternal* is the law of God's being, the law to which God himself works. For humankind this law is manifested in several other kinds of law, which together form a hierarchy.
- *The angelic law* is the law for angels.
- *The law of reason* binds all things together. Every person is created with the capacity within themselves to follow a path which will express the purpose of their creation.

Humanity is unique within creation in having a choice as to whether or not we fulfil the particular purpose for which each of us is created, or whether we choose to question or to deviate from the creator's purpose for us. Thus 'reason' is not just the human capacity to think. It is something in us given by God, the light that lightens every person who is created (in the words of the prologue to John's gospel). This God-given faculty is the potential in each person to discover who they are and what they should become to fulfil the eternal law of God's purposes and processes.

- *The divine law* is God's special revelation through Scripture. God can speak to us through Scripture to inspire and enlighten reason, and to reveal things beyond our normal ability to think and to understand.
- *Human law* is what human beings devise on the basis of divine law and the law of reason, to express what we are about and how we should be, to order human affairs so as to better fulfil the purposes of God.
- *Natural law* is that which determines the paths of other, lower beings.

EXERCISE

What are the strengths and weaknesses of Hooker's notion of laws?

'Reason is not just the human capacity to think – it is something in us given by God.' How do you understand 'reason' and its place in the journeying of this life?

In what sense does Scripture contain 'all that is necessary to salvation'?

How the laws work

This hierarchy of laws is based on two important ideas. First, Hooker takes from Aristotle the notion of correspondence. Any of these types of law must correspond to God's purposes for himself and his creation in his law. Each type of law will correspond to the law eternal. Thus, for example, human laws are good in that the eternal law 'worketh in them'.

In this way God's supreme purposes are mediated to humankind and we are able to discern and express what, in the language of the second collect at Evening Prayer, is 'good' and 'just' and 'holy'.

Moreover, the whole of created life is pregnant with God-given potential and the human task is to discover, receive and use the various types of law so that this potential can be most fully realised. Every law we make, every decision, everything we organise, has the potential to be in the image of God's eternal purpose and thus to help us to be on the way to fulfilling that purpose: though, in this life, Hooker recognises the perspective of 1 Corinthians 13:11–13, 'my knowledge now is partial – then it will be whole' (*New English Bible*).

Within this process, which requires struggle, discernment and development, everything is potentially part of God's purpose and God's way of working. Everything can participate in the mind of God. Here is a theological underpinning of the inclusiveness of Anglican theology. Further, the notion of law meant that for Hooker the whole world has an *order*, which must be properly discerned and acknowledged so as to lead to a deeper knowledge of God and a better fulfilment of God's purposes. This notion of law stresses potential, growth and change. It is something dynamic rather than something set, restrictive and controlling in a negative sense (which is how we usually understand 'law' today). The visible, fleshly world of human being provides a basis for knowledge of the invisible working and will of God.

The second key idea for the unity of the hierarchy of laws also comes from Aristotle. This is the idea of 'appropriateness'. As we work at the process of living, whatever we receive through God's light in us and around us, or through the special revelation of Scripture, to allow us to try to fulfil the proper potential of every creature to become what God wants it to become, can be measured by 'appropriateness'. In our sinfulness and imperfection we have a tendency to deviate from what is properly appropriate, from a close correspondence with the law eternal. We are tempted not to want to become what God wants us to become, but to become something else. Appropriateness is 'that which is fitting' in the world *God* has created.

Here Hooker is holding together two things:

- he recognises the sinfulness of humanity, a theme that was central to puritan theology; and
- he recognises that humanity and creation are full of goodness – the appropriate potential to become what God has made them to be. This theme reflects the greater optimism of catholic theology.

Thus humanity is not totally flawed. We are imperfect and sinful, but we have the potential in us for God's laws to speak to us through reason and revelation so that we can appropriately fulfil God's purposes. All good things are of God, but there is a very real choice for human beings and thus there is a key place for discipline, struggle and development.

EXERCISE
📖 **Read Acts 2:17–21.**

What might be seen as signs of correspondence and appropriateness in this text?

How can modern Christian life seek a proper correspondence and appropriateness in relation to God's will today?

Discerning the framework

Hooker states that God's wisdom is known in four things:

> Wisdom hath diversely imparted her treasure unto the world. As her ways are of sundry kinds, so her measure of teaching is not merely one and the same. Some things she openeth by the sacred books of Scripture; some things by the glorious work of Nature: with some things she inspireth from above by spiritual influence; in some things she leadeth and traineth only by worldly experience and practice. (Hooker, 1907, p. 237)

Thus we have a number of resources through which we can identify God's wisdom:

- Scripture, through which we can know the will and wisdom of God;
- Nature – for the creation is pregnant with what God has created it to be (this challenged both catholic and puritan tendencies to denigrate Nature);

- the inspiration of God, through which some great spiritual truth or influence is made known to us; and
- our experience in the world – this is the germ of our recognition that the secular and the 'non-Christian' can speak to us of God.

By exploring the world in which we are set, and our own choices and aspirations, we can learn something of God's laws and thus the potential for each part of our lives. Everything has an appropriate potential to become what it should and the purpose of creation is for all these things to work harmoniously to become one in the greater whole that is God. Thus everything and every person has the potential for goodness and the fulfilment of God's purposes. Our task is to discern what is right for ourselves, our family, our group, our society: discerning how each element can most appropriately correspond to God's will.

Insights come from Scripture, Nature, spiritual inspiration and experience of the world. All these things can feed us and there is a necessary dynamic relationship between them. Scripture is primary but only in relation to the other elements of revelation. Wisdom and truth do not come simply from Scripture but also from Nature, spiritual inspiration and experience of the world; as there is a correspondence between each of these elements all must accord with Scripture.

Hooker's hierarchy of laws means that there will be a harmony between these four sources of revelation and in the direction we receive from them, with regard both to the law eternal and to our attempts to explore this in terms of the law of reason, divine law, human law and natural law.

The reality of our struggle to discern what is appropriate is recognised by Hooker's reference to the centrality of the suffering Christ: his cross and his bloodshed. Hooker acknowledges that the human ability to fight against the call to realise our proper potential is very powerful and costs God dearly. Yet in Christ we have a picture of God entering into human experience and of humanity being perfectly inspired by God to fulfil his purposes. Christ shows us the cost and the way of discerning the potential of creation and of each part within it. He also shows us how all the parts must be drawn together in God's oneness. Jesus' vision of the Kingdom was about a corporation. Paul's great teaching about the body is also about a corporation in which all things will find their proper place and part. Hooker is realistic about crucifixion being part of the process for humankind; his account of laws was not simply a neat theory, there was a ready acknowledgement of our in-built tendency to fight against the call of the creator's potential and to cause pain to ourselves and to God.

Hooker writes: 'And his Church he frameth out of the very flesh, the very wounded and bleeding side of the Son of man' (Hooker, Book V, LVI, 7; 1907, Vol. 2, p. 229). For this reason the word preached and the sacraments of baptism and Eucharist are essential, because these are the ways in which we participate most profoundly in the law eternal and measure the correspondence and appropriateness of our own attempts to discern laws. The word of God is given in Scripture. Baptism cleanses and invites fuller participation: it lays the foundation and attains 'the first beginning of a new life'. Holy Communion remakes fellowship with God and with each other: it provides 'nourishment and food prescribed for continuance of life' (Hooker, Book V, LVII, 1; 1907, Vol. 2, p. 319).

Here is the supreme measure and guide for human being, since to be fulfilled each person needs to do two things. First, we need to participate with one another within creation and therefore we have to be always growing in fellowship in oneness with others. Second, we have to participate more in the life of God. These things come together in worship, which is a binding together of people before and in God. Therefore *The Book of Common Prayer* is central to Hooker's thinking and the task of the public ministry is to do those two things:
- to help people to bind together and realise their potential in the body and in the corporateness of what we have been created to be;
- to do that as expressing our worship of God.

The tools of this ministry are Scripture and the two sacraments, which connect the reality of our struggles and imperfection with the generosity of God's grace and outreach to us.

Participation

Hooker bases this theology on a doctrine of participation. He uses the phrase 'participation for edification' and proclaims, 'God is in Christ, Christ is in us, we are in Him.' The individual is incomplete. We require completion through communion with God and with the oneness of God's creation, that is through participation in Christ.

This is an important and distinguishing feature of sixteenth-century Anglicanism. The key doctrines of continental Christianity were justification (Luther), the sovereignty of God (Calvin) and the sovereignty of the Church (Roman Catholicism). Hooker emphasised 'purifying by participation'. As we participate with others more fully in God's purposes, and as we thus participate more fully in the life and laws of God himself, so we are purified and grow more fully into what we are called to become. Participation with others and with God are the tasks of public ministry; both are radically inclusive. The ordained are agents of this participation. Moreover, such participation is essentially dynamic and active: 'the continual intercourse' of angels descending from heaven with doctrine ('heavenly inspirations') and ascending with prayer ('holy desires'), incorporating us into that society that has Jesus Christ as its head and together with him makes one body.

EXERCISE
📖 Read *Of The Laws of Ecclesiastical Polity*, Book V, section LXVII.

'The extra-ordinary: the ordinary in the extraordinary.' Can you recognise this insight in the life of your own Church and its handling of the sacraments of participation – baptism and communion?

Hooker identifies four resources for identifying God's wisdom: Scripture, Nature, inspiration, human experience. How do we handle these resources today?

Scripture, reason and tradition

Hooker gives valuable guidance about the use of Scripture, reason and tradition.

Scripture is primary

In the language of the Thirty-Nine Articles, this claim is expressed in these terms:

> Article VI. *Of the Sufficiency of the holy Scriptures for salvation:*
> Holy Scripture containeth all things necessary to salvation: so that whatsoever is not read therein, nor may be proved thereby, is not required of any man, that it should be believed as an article of the Faith, or be thought requisite or necessary to salvation.

Scripture helps us to see the laws by which we are called to live but it does not give us detail for our own time. The continuing development of God-given potential means that we have to wrestle with Scripture in order to translate it and to use it appropriately. Thus Hooker agrees with Gregory the Great (see Chapter 1) that issues such as how the Church should be governed, its ceremonies and the form of its liturgy may well change from time to time and from place to place.

To use Scripture appropriately we need to exercise reason. This is the God-given faculty human beings possess which allows us to discover the truth that God wishes to reveal in Scripture, in Nature and through inspiration.

Reason

Reason is more than the human ability to think; it is a special faculty. Reason is exercised by those who are, in Hooker's words, 'of God'. This emphasis is especially important because, in pastoral terms, Anglicanism includes everyone. Each person has the potential to fulfil God's particular purposes for themselves, and thus in relation to their own context. However, not everyone will contribute equally to the discerning of truth and appropriateness. God calls and commissions particular people to particular roles and tasks in the exercise of 'reason' – always in relation to the whole community but often on its behalf. Thus the authority of reason as given by God will be aristocratic rather than democratic: all will have a contribution, but some will be more significant for the wellbeing of the whole than others.

Reason will operate by measuring correspondence and appropriateness, using the resources of Scripture, Nature, experience of life and inspiration.

Thus reason will not provide absolute or infallible answers, but rather what is appropriate at that time and in that place and stage, in and through which we are called to fulfil our potential. Because the outcome of the exercise of reason will be appropriate to the time and place, it will provide the seeds of diversity rather than of a narrow uniformity.

Tradition

This is seen by Hooker to be the least important of the three basic ingredients to discernment. It is important to accumulate human experience of the grace of God, since this provides precious clues about the structures and styles of God's operation to which we must correspond. But the ongoing development of our God-given potential means that we must guard against the discernment of the past becoming a straight-jacket which inhibits further growth.

Scripture and reason are likely to be sources of new insight and challenge, which may on occasion require us to take further what has already been learned.

A modern example of this approach would be the speech of the Bishop of Guildford, the Rt Revd Michael Adie, in the debate in the General Synod of the Church of England in November 1992 about the ordination of women to the priesthood. He argued that this step was a proper *development* of tradition, under the guidance of God, in accord with Scripture and God-given reason (General Synod, 1992, pp. 704–707). This claim that tradition must change and grow is classic Anglicanism.

Hooker insists that the Church is not infallible and perfect: we need 'to reform ourselves if at any time we have done amiss' (Hooker, Book III, I, 10; 1907, Vol. 1, p. 292). For Hooker the mind of the Church and the norm of catholicity is the transmission of certain living qualities of faith and order, not the transmission of set forms. Thus tradition is essentially dynamic, evolving from ongoing reflection by the Church on her experiences past and present. 'Consensus' is something that grows from conflict ('fundamentalisms in dialogue') and will ever regrow from the Church struggling with the dynamic interrelation of:

• redeemed reason, articulated by those who are 'of God';
• the tradition of wisdom, accumulated by the Church in her history;
• Scripture as central and controlling;
• the corporation of the faithful and their experience of a God-given life and call;
• the context provided by the whole community – God's life and call in creation.

This consensus and 'mind' is dynamic, uneven, always emerging. It is located in collegiality and not in individual, monarchical authority.

The Church

This means that Hooker is realistic about the Church, which will always be a 'mixed bunch' but with the potential to become more fully part of God's purposes. Some members will exercise God-given reason for the benefit of the whole (an idea later developed more fully by Charles Gore – see Chapter 7) but in relation to, and as part of, the whole community, its context and its use of the resources of Scripture and tradition.

This contrasts with the continental confidence in the infallibility of the Church, either in its officers or its Scriptures or its teaching. For Hooker, the Church lives and grows and changes and develops because of a dynamic between all these ingredients. Yet, as always, there is a strong sense of realism, for he recognises that even when the most careful method is most judiciously employed it yields at best only the highest probability that can humanly be achieved and is never beyond further debate. Moreover, conflict to engender consensus is costly: the crucifixion stands as the supreme sign of the tension between the highest ideals, the reality of human sinfulness and the miraculousness of grace that comes as light from darkness. Hooker writes:

> What merit, force or virtue soever there is in his sacrificed body and blood, we freely fully and wholly have it by this sacrament [of Holy Communion] ... the effect thereof in us is a real transmutation of our souls and bodies from sin to righteousness, from death and corruption to immortality and life. (Hooker, Book V, LXVII, 7; 1907, Vol. 2, p. 325)

Hence sacraments are means of participating in this process of transformation.

The dynamic of change, development and growth presupposes conflict and cost. Again Hooker is realistic: in recognising and pursuing conflict it may be 'that suspense of judgment and exercise of charity were safer and seemlier for Christian men, than the hot pursuit of ... controversies' (Hooker, Book IV, XIV, 6; 1907, Vol. 1, p. 427). Authority does not lie in the infallibility of Pope or Church (Catholic), Scripture (Protestantism) or reason (liberal), but in the integrity of this dialogue – which may be thought of as 'fundamentalisms in dialogue'. 'Think ye are men, deem it not impossible for you to err; sift unpartially your own hearts, whether it be force of reason or vehemency of affection, which hath bred and still doth feed these opinions in you' (Hooker, Preface; 1907, Vol. 1, p. 143).

The 'mind' of the Christian Church will ever regrow from the dynamic interaction of redeemed reason (articulated particularly by those who are 'of God'), the tradition of wisdom, Scripture as central and controlling, the corporation of all the faithful and their experiences of God-given life and call, and the context provided by the whole community.

EXERCISE

How can Scripture be 'central and controlling' in our Christian life?

Are any of these ingredients missing in your own experience of trying to make a local Church?

How can we understand Hooker's concern that only some are called 'of God' to articulate 'reason': that is that authority in the Church will be aristocratic, not democratic?

How do you react to these kinds of insight about how a Church can be inclusive and yet operate within a clear framework, especially by means of a process of fundamentalisms in dialogue, where conflict and cost will be necessary and yet creative? How does this thinking relate to your own reflections on the relationship of an individual to a group?

📖 **Read Acts 2:22–42.** What might the passage say about:
- the person of Jesus in relation to goodness, sin, crucifixion, resurrection (vv. 22–24);
- the use of Scripture (vv. 29–31);
- God-given 'reason' (vv. 32–36);
- the sacraments of cleansing and feeding (vv. 37–42);
- the relationship between all these elements?

Further reading

Avis, P (1989), *Anglicanism and the Christian Church*, Edinburgh, T and T Clark.

Booty, J (1987), The judicious Mr Hooker and authority in the Elizabethan Church, in S Sykes (ed.), *Authority in the Anglican Communion*, chapter 6, Toronto, Anglican Book Centre.

Grislis, E (1963), Richard Hooker's method of theological inquiry, *Anglican Theological Review*, 45, 190–203.

Hylson-Smith, K (1996), *The Churches in England from Elizabeth I to Elizabeth II: Vol I, 1558–1688*, London, SCM.

Marshall, J S (1963), *Hooker and the Anglican Tradition*, London, A and C Black.

McAdoo, H (1992), Richard Hooker, in G Rowell (ed.), *The English Religious Tradition and the Genius of Anglicanism*, chapter 6, Wantage, IKON.

Speed Hill, W (ed.) (1972), *Studies in Richard Hooker*, London, The Press of Case Western Reserve Library.

Wolf, W J (ed.) (1979), *The Spirit of Anglicanism*, Wilton, Connecticut, Morehouse-Barlow.

3. SHAPING A TRADITION

Introduction

At the end of the sixteenth century, Hooker developed a theological framework for the emerging Church of England. In the next century George Herbert became an icon of the pastoral and priestly practice that gave particular substance to this framework, and which has been the bedrock of subsequent Anglican ecclesiology, focused in the parish system as the local manifestation of the catholic Church.

Reflecting on experience

Think of a case of bereavement, in your own life or in that of someone you know. What can the Church offer at such times and what can the Church receive? Consider issues of:
- ritual;
- place;
- the ministry;
- hope and fear;
- the personal and the universal.

EXERCISE

📖 **Read Acts 2:43–47.** What can we learn from this passage about the nature of Christian community and the resources offered to it? You might like to consider:
- the role of apostles;
- the place of inspiration;
- mutuality and pastoral care;
- the temple as public meeting place for common worship;
- house communion;
- salvation as gift, yet needing to be located in a community;
- the importance of a sense of awe.

George Herbert (1593–1633)

George Herbert was educated at Trinity College, Cambridge where he became a tutor in 1618. In the following year he was appointed Public Orator for the University. In 1624 he was elected MP for Montgomery and began a political career. He had long struggled with a sense of vocation to ordained ministry, however, and in December that year he was made deacon. In 1629 he married Jane Danvers and it was his marriage to her which seems to have freed him finally to relinquish his political aspirations in favour of ministry in the Church. That fact is a sign of an important 'earthiness' and a pointer towards his approach to the Christian life.

On 19 September 1630, Herbert was ordained priest in Salisbury Cathedral and six months later he was presented to the living of Bemerton, a small village near Salisbury. On 1 March 1633 he died. Though he was a parish priest for only three years, in this short time he provided a profound example of a style of Anglican ministry and spirituality which expressed Hooker's inclusive framework in a local setting. Some of the ingredients from this short ministry can help to indicate the shaping of the Anglican tradition which Herbert provided.

Starting with yourself: Twice a week Herbert used to walk into Salisbury to attend worship in the Cathedral. He called it his heaven on earth. If he was going to nourish others, he needed appropriate nourishment himself. Each person has their particular spiritual needs.

A sense of unworthiness and humility: Herbert remained a deacon for six years. He struggled with his vocation. His poetry illustrates a profound sense of unworthiness and humility.

'Jesus Christ my master': This is a very important phrase for Herbert. One of the reasons he chose to become parish priest of such a small village was in order to declare his loyalty to Christ his master. If he had sought a prestigious living, or political office, that would have compromised his loyalty because he knew he would be tempted to enjoy such things for their own sake. 'Jesus Christ my master' was a powerful challenge to worldly or ecclesiastical ambition. God was met and served in the small scale and the ordinary.

The power of Scripture: Herbert was devoted to the Bible. He made extensive use of biblical language and images.

The discipline of the Church: This is the focus for worship in the community. All personal prayer and human exploration is subordinate to the rhythm and discipline of the worship of the Church. This is why he placed such high value on the daily offices as public events.

A deep personal struggle with God: He was very honest in his writing and preaching about moments of doubt and times of testing. He recognised the place of struggle and darkness in human life – as with the years of doubt and exploration before his ordination. Herbert was open enough to struggle and to question.

The tradition of the Fathers: Herbert valued the teaching of the Church Fathers. He recognised that besides rooting Christian living in the Scripture and in reflection upon the present, there is much that has happened in between from which we can learn. Most fruitful and formative were the teachings of the Fathers. This is a classically Anglican approach to theology; for Herbert his praying and his pastoring required rootedness in what God had given to the Church.

Seven whole days not one in seven: God is concerned with the whole of life. Besides Scripture, tradition and Church life, the world was full of God's power and purpose. Everything and everyone in the locality was part of God's purpose and the concern of the parish church.

A high doctrine of priesthood and of Eucharist: This is evident in his own journey and in his personal prayer life. He wrote an important manual, *The Country Parson*, which established the pastoral and priestly nature of public ministry. This was especially important as the abolition of the monasteries, chantries and minor orders at the Reformation meant that all key public ministerial tasks now fell to the parish priest.

Change, division and disruption are to be expected: Herbert was realistic about the fact that change, division and disruption are part and parcel of the Christian life. There was no cosy plateau to which to ascend and live in safety.

EXERCISE
Choose two of the ingredients given above and say why you think
that they are important today.

Which marks of Herbert's approach to ministry are least helpful?
What are your reasons for choosing them?

Making the Church: a parochial identity

One of Herbert's most basic concepts is that of a truly parochial spirituality. He believed that the ordinary parish church could become the
true centre of Christian community, even though not everybody attended. Those who came together to pray did so as a sacrament of the
prayerfulness of everyone in the parish.

This parochial spirituality is rooted in a number of key factors. From
the human point of view there is always a struggle to know God and to
be open to God. Yet each person is made with the instinct to pray: to
hope, to regret, to wonder. The task of the Church is to offer opportunities for this basic human instinct to be expressed appropriately and
connected to the one who fulfils human hopefulness and forgives
human failings.

Another key factor is that God is one. Everyone in the community is
called to participate in the oneness of God, enacted in the worship of the
body of Christ in each place. Only in the community of God's Church
can peace, truth and glory be fully known, through 'Jesus my master'.

Such factors feature in Herbert's poetry. There is an emphasis there
upon everyday objects and images, and the humanness through which
we struggle to know God, as well as a faith in the sacrament of God's
presence in ordinary things, which becomes a sign that they are part of
a greater whole that only God holds together. The Church is seen as the
place for this participation in God's oneness, with the Scripture as the
text for expressing and exploring this reality and the ministry provided
to oversee the invitation and the response to this Gospel.

EXERCISE
How does this notion of parochial spirituality link with your earlier reflections about the Church and about bereavement?

God's spiritual power: the clue to human maturity and salvation

In his book *The Country Parson*, Herbert wrote of 'the great aptness that country people have to think that all things come by a kind of natural course and that if they sow their ground they must have corn. Therefore their labours prevent them from seeing God's hand in all this' (1956, p. 73). In most of life, people expect natural processes together with their own efforts to furnish all that they require.

Herbert argued that we must recognise that God exercises what he called a sustaining power, a governing power and a spiritual power. In appreciating these things we can learn how to bring to light the life of prayer and thus see our endeavours in this world in a proper perspective.

The sustaining power is that by which 'God preserves and actuates everything in his being so that corn does not grow by any other virtue.' God gives life to everything (as Hooker established with his notion of laws). The spiritual life begins by our learning to appreciate this profound truth. In terms of the passage from Acts, we may think of developing a proper sense of 'awe' and acknowledging the larger and more mysterious context in which we are set.

With regard to *God's governing power*, Herbert writes:

> God preserves and orders the references of things to one another so that although the corn does grow and be preserved by this sustaining power yet if He suits not other things to the growth, like seasons and weather and other accidents, by his governing power, the governing power of all things, then the fairest harvest will come to nothing. (1956, p. 74).

God not only sustains all things. God governs the inter-relationship of all things. Both of these facts form the basis of Christian prayer. Herbert's point about God's governing power links with Hooker and later Laud (see Chapter 4), stressing the interdependence of things in the tradition of Aristotle. For Herbert this inter-dependence under God is the key context in which the Christian prays and lives. The Church is commissioned to help people own both their dependence on God's governing power and their interdependence under God. Liturgy and pastoral ministry provide the means for this task to be undertaken in each locality. Most of us could recognise this foundation for spiritual life, in exploring God's sustaining power and his governing power. Many of those who turn to the Church in times of need or of celebration recognise these forces.

Herbert goes on to write of *God's spiritual power*. 'It is observable that God delights to have men feel and acknowledge and reverence His power, and therefore He often overturns things when they are thought past danger' (1956, p. 74). In the spiritual life we sometimes relax in knowing God's sustaining power and governing power and so God brings stress, challenge or disaster to pull us out of any complacency and to ensure that we really know our dependence upon him. This is God's spiritual power: a power that is exercised to overturn the complacency which the spiritual life often attains when it concentrates upon God's sustaining and governing power, by challenging us to recognise the essentially mysterious and ever-growing and changing process of God. The temptation of the spiritual life is to use prayer as a means of domesticating this power into categories of sustenance and government, which soon become constraints of human order and perception. God is known most challengingly through the spiritual power by which we are surprised, cast down or overturned.

The Old Testament catalogues Israel's development of a spirituality that recognised God's sustaining power and governing power, but which tended to capture this awareness and exploration in rituals and laws. The result was that God constantly exercises his spiritual power, bringing disaster, upset and challenge so as to open people to greater possibilities and new life through the breaking up of the familiar moulds that we tend to construct to domesticate our experiences of grace. Herbert recognised that God exercises spiritual power so that people 'should perpetuate and not break off their acts of dependence'. He writes, 'God's goodness strives with man's refactoriness, man would sit down at this world: God bids him sell it and purchase a better' (1956, p. 75).

EXERCISE

Can you think of examples from Scripture of these different forms of God's power?

Many people know from their own experience the truth that when pain and pressure disrupt our lives, prayer and openness to new things comes most profoundly, if inarticulately. Can you recall any examples from your own life?

In what ways can the Church invite people to recognise this path of prayer? (Does Acts 2:43–47 give any clues?)

The parish church and the life of prayer

For Herbert, the parish church is the place for the life of prayer to be focused and sustained. He gives us a number of reasons.

The importance of the pastor

Herbert has a high doctrine of priesthood. He maintains the traditional Christian theology that humankind fell from fellowship with God through disobedience. Christ is the instrument of God for what Herbert calls 'the revoking of human life' that is to restore us. But 'Christ being not continual on earth, that after He had fulfilled the work of reconciliation to be received up into heaven, He constituted deputies in His place, and these are priests' (Herbert, 1956, p. 12). The minister is called to stand in Christ's place, to call people to the Gospel and to administer his sacraments. This is a key measuring rod for each life of prayer – both in giving focus and in offering the assurance of forgiveness and restoration for any falling short.

The place of Scripture

The parish church is the place where Scripture is read and explored for each individual and for the whole community. Herbert says that there are four things in Scripture:
• precepts for life;
• doctrines for knowledge;
• examples for illustration;
• promises for comfort.

These elements of Scripture inform our prayer. An essential part of the spiritual life is comparing scripture with scripture – a work that can be done by the individual, but a work that is done for all believers by the scholars and teachers of the Church. Herbert writes that just as one country 'does not bear all things, that there may be commerce, so neither has God opened, or will open all to one, that there may be a traffic in knowledge between the servants of God, for the planting of both love and humility' (1956, p. 18).

The importance of charity

The parish church is a focus for charity: for helping each Christian life relate to others in a generous and loving way. Herbert gives the example of the pastor who 'keeps his money for the poor and his table for those who are above alms . . . not that the poor are not welcomed to his table, but often he chooses to give the poor money which they can better employ to their own advantage and suitability of their needs than so much given in meat at dinner' (1956, pp. 36–37).

This is our modern 'Christian Aid' principle of giving money to the poor so that they can decide best how to meet their own needs, rather than simply receiving food from the tables of the rich. In this way Herbert sees two things in the Church as important as a focus for Christian charity:

The importance of friendship and hospitality: We receive the life of God in social relationships, community life and shared meals. The parish church is the place where this truth can be known most clearly.

The centrality of justice: Those in real need should be given the means to order their own lives rather than coming to and receiving charity at another's table.

In these ways the Church acts to encourage goodness (and goodness is a sign of, and a call to, recognising God's life amongst us) besides being a forerunner of that great goodness which is eternity. For Herbert, the parish church is a model of Christian community, of how God has created the world to be. It is spirituality in action. Thus the Church should take care that there 'should not be a beggar or idle person in our parish but all should be in a competent way of getting their living' (Herbert, 1956, p. 38).

The place of pastoral work

Herbert recognised the importance of Christians being alongside others in their need. Although he writes as a pastor, his wisdom has application for all who strive to live the Christian life. He says that we must try to help people see that their life is sustained and governed by God. Thus everyday life is important. The disturbances and challenges in everyday life may be special revelations of God's 'spiritual power' whereby people can most profoundly acknowledge their dependence upon God.

Thus pastoral work has to have an edge. It is not simply a matter of being kind to people in their needs and asking, 'How are you?' This tends to be our modern style – to build a pastoral relationship through listening skills exercised around that question, allowing the other to work out their own way of handling things, and making an implicit witness to God's love by the Christian visitor offering qualities of care and concern. Herbert was clear that the Christian Gospel offered much more than kindness and a therapy to encourage people to learn how better to handle their own salvation. He recognised that most people in need are already surrounded by others, family and neighbours, who are constantly asking, 'How are you?' and thus administering this basic human cocktail of care and a prod to therapeutic self-awareness.

The Christian pastoral visitor represents a Gospel and a Church which stands for much more. When the Christian has pastoral contact, the key questions for Herbert are not of the 'How are you?' variety. Rather, the Christian comes to ask other questions.

• Are you saying your prayers?
• Are you reading the Scriptures?
• Are you teaching the faith to your children?

With the sick, Herbert argues, the Christian should always speak about Christ's suffering, God's care and the fact that all of us need completion in him. The Christian visitor might mention the medicine of holy communion.

The point of pastoral work is to try to offer – and draw out from others – a deeper spirituality which constitutes a clearer awareness that God sustains and governs and is present in the problems and tests of life. God calls us into that dependence which can trust in the fulfilment we call eternity. The message of the Christian carer is that God is trying to draw people to himself through all the joyful and dreadful things that make up the mixture of life.

The parish church is the essential context for Christian caring that is rooted in such an understanding of spirituality.

The importance of faith and justice in a suffering world

Herbert was very realistic about suffering in the world. One example is his advice about how to react if God has sent some calamity, such as fire or famine, to a neighbouring parish. In a world of limited mobility this would be Herbert's equivalent of facing the question of how to react to the suffering which pours into our lives through the media. News of suffering elsewhere demands a certain kind of response.

First, the Christian community should come together. Response is through the corporation of the Church, not through the individual. Then those who come together must be 'exposed to learn from the calamity about the uncertainty of human affairs'. 'Who might be next?' he asks. The community begins by opening itself to what he has called God's spiritual power – that disturbance of the sustaining and governing powers with which we try to be in quiet harmony. The result will be that the community will be 'affrighted'. There is a proper fear of the Lord to be recognised in confronting any kind of human 'disaster'.

There follows 'the obligation of charity'. Christians come together, recognise what has happened, acknowledge the uncertainty of human affairs, our own frailty, a proper fear of the Lord; and the outcome is an obligation of charity to those who are suffering. Thus Christians must 'give liberally', in whatever way is appropriate. Further, Christians must incite others to give help. When a 'sum' has been assembled it should be sent, or better we should all find some day together when we can walk over to that village and give the gift in person. This contact makes clear the oneness of givers and receivers.

This is a powerful sequence for enfleshing the spiritual life in relation to the sufferings of others: a response which is grounded in the corporation of the Church and a community sequence of sharing information, deepening a spiritual response, recognising our own frailty and dependence, and acting together to emphasise our oneness with those in need.

The place of the sacraments

Christian faith is a living, dynamic, growing phenomenon. The spiritual life is where we work at this call to grow and a key ingredient is the sacraments held by the Church for all Christ's children. Thus, for Herbert, in the life of prayer we should regularly recall our baptism. This provides the principles by which we can grow. Similarly, holy communion is a place of knowing our need, our incompleteness and the miracle of God's grace. It requires careful preparation. Herbert's poem 'Love Bade Me Welcome' expresses this most eloquently. Holy communion is the eating together of the parish, which is its participation in Christ.

EXERCISE

📖 **Read 'Love Bade Me Welcome'.** Does Herbert's poem express your own theology?

> Love bade me welcome; yet my soul drew back,
>   Guilty of dust and sin.
> But quick-eyed Love, observing me grow slack
>   From my first entrance in,
> Drew nearer to me, sweetly questioning,
>   If I lacked anything.

'A guest', I answered, 'worthy to be here.'
 Love said, 'You shall be he.'
'I, the unkind, ungrateful? Ah, my dear,
 I cannot look on thee.'
Love took my hand, and smiling did reply,
 'Who made the eyes but I?'

'Truth, Lord, but I have marred them; let my shame
 Go where it doth deserve.'
'And know you not', says Love, 'who bore the blame?'
 'My dear, then I will serve.'
'You must sit down', says Love, 'and taste my meat.'
 So I did sit and eat.

The place of humility and trust in God

Each person receives what Herbert calls 'the darts of the unfriendly'. When things go wrong, people criticise or challenge. The Church is there to call Christians to respond with humility and 'unconcern for ourselves'. On our own we are most likely to seek revenge or retreat into ourselves; the Church provides a wider perspective and hopefulness, where we can be strengthened and supported to suffer, to trust in God's power and purposes and to act in ways which have been tested by fellowship with others.

Public prayer in the community

This is seen as the measure and nourisher of all that has gone before.

EXERCISE

The parish church is the place for the life of prayer to be focused and sustained. Which of Herbert's reasons for this assertion are most challenging for us today, and why?

How would you assess his views about pastoral work and spirituality?

Public worship: the parish church as a model for the whole community

Herbert instigated a pattern of saying morning and evening prayer daily in the parish church at Bemerton. Often it was his family and servants who constituted the congregation. However, his reflections on this discipline of public worship provide insights into the way in which the parish church can be a model and a mediator for the whole community in which it is set.

In his book *The Rule of Holy Life*, Herbert states that spirituality is based on three things: tradition, Scripture and agriculture (Davies, 1975, p. 103). Christian life should be based on whatever could be learned from engaging with tradition, and the teaching and wisdom of the Church. This provides a system of God-given order. Similarly, it should be based on whatever could be learned from engaging with Scripture, the word of God which speaks to each person in his or her uniqueness. This is a focus on God's particular revelation. And Christian life should be based on 'agriculture', that is taking seriously the life of the world in which we are set, which for Herbert was a small farming community. Public worship was the place to explore each of these three ingredients and their interrelationships.

The way of exercising this method was by observing the rhythm of daily morning and evening prayer. Twice each day, Herbert and his family walked across to Bemerton Church, where he rang the church bell as an invitation and a sign to the whole community. Public worship was not just for those who attended; it was for the whole community. Herbert practised a parochial spirituality. It was not important who came or how many attended. What was important was that the worship happened publicly, in the heart of the community. Prayer was practised through Jesus my master, the crucified redeemer.

In the offices of morning and evening prayer we find the mix of the three ingredients Herbert required for Christian spirituality (see Walton, 1973, pp. 295–302). The creeds and canticles represent the wisdom and teaching of the Church. The authority of the Church was symbolised by the bishop, and by the minister as the bishop's local representative. These ingredients for certainty were the fruits and seeds of what the Church has been given to 'know': the wisdom that is to be part and parcel of every occasion of public praying.

The Scriptures are read systematically: God's word speaking to each individual who hears. This is a word to be trusted and obeyed – ingredients for certainty about God, his Christ and the Gospel.

The offices began with the public ringing of the church bell and ended with prayers, both set prayers and a time for other prayer also. Here was the place for Herbert's 'agriculture' (Walton, 1973, p. 301): the concerns and hopes and fears of the actual community. Here the spirituality of struggle was placed next to the ingredients provided by Church and Bible. Praying the community's concerns in this context provided the ingredients for knowing and not knowing, believing and not believing, certainty and struggle. Here was a daily framework for the interaction of God's gifts, through Church and Scripture, with the real lives of the community. The daily offices confront 'private' prayer with public and ecclesial concerns, and each individual life is to be rooted in this interaction through which the living Spirit of God speaks and acts. Individual concerns are given space as part of the wider praying after the third collect and in the moment of reflection that can be occasioned by people stopping to acknowledge the ringing of the church bell for worship. In these ways individual concerns are challenged not to become indulgent or escapist, for they are clearly part of corporate prayer, and the processes of private and public devotion are daily confronted by what is given and known in tradition and in Scripture (Walton, 1973, p. 301).

The discipline of daily offices, observed in the parish church but conjoining all who live in that place, is a model whereby individual spirituality is continually tested and broadened by the wider context of public concerns and God's teaching in tradition and Scripture. Here is a method for Christian praying which makes parochial spirituality primary and in which each person is invited to find an appropriate place and pattern.

In this sense, spirituality is not about rules and rituals based on what the Church knows and Scripture teaches. Spirituality is about a relationship with the living God, using what God has given as trustworthy but exploring present possibilities and perplexities too, always open to new leadings and new promptings but firmly rooted in what has been given.

EXERCISE

What do you think of the idea of a 'method' in prayer that requires fixed creeds and canticles, set Scripture readings, public affairs and private concerns? To what extent is this a framework for a genuinely parochial spirituality?

Does our modern emphasis upon eucharistic worship enhance or inhibit Herbert's ideals for the daily offices?

The Church as local, priestly and pastoral: a praying community

For Herbert, the parish was not simply a geographical area. It was a recognised space within which the prayer that lives in each human being can be given appropriate focus and direction. This essential task requires a holy place, a structure for worship and an authorised person.

These elements are not the essential ingredients of a parish, however. The essential ingredient is the life of prayer in that place: human spirituality owned, focused, challenged and directed.

EXERCISE

📖 **Read Acts 3:1–10.** What might we learn about pastoral and priestly ministry from this account? Consider especially:

- the hour for prayer (v. 1) and the discipline of daily public prayer;
- the location at the temple – a special holy place;
- the lame man who seeks pastoral care and support from worshippers;
- Peter offering neither material help nor kind words, but wholeness in Jesus Christ. It is in the mystery of the crucified, the testing of humanness, that new life is given;
- the response of walking and praising God – journeying in surprise and amazement. There are no satisfying answers but only the continuing question, 'What does this mean?';
- struggle and challenge are not annulled, but continue.

Further reading

Clarke, E (1992), George Herbert's *The Temple*: the Genius of Anglicanism and the inspiration for poetry, in G Rowell (ed.), *The English Religious Tradition and the Genius of Anglicanism*, chapter 7, Wantage, IKON.

Herbert, G (1956), *The Country Parson and Selected Poems*, London, SCM.

Moorman, J R H (1983), *The Anglican Spiritual Tradition*, London, Darton, Longman and Todd.

Thornton, M (1963), *English Spirituality*, London, SPCK.

Van de Weyer, R (1989), *Lament and Love: the vision of George Herbert*, London, Lamp Press.

Wolf, W J (ed.) (1982), *Anglican Spirituality*, Wilton, Connecticut, Morehouse-Barlow.

4. SHAPING A NATIONAL CHURCH

Introduction

Hooker and Herbert established key markers in terms of a theological framework, and in terms of pastoral and priestly practice rooted in the parochial system. In the midst of the tensions that led to the Civil War in England and the apparent overthrow of Anglicanism, William Laud developed a robust but open understanding of the structures and style essential to the survival of a flexible and coherent national Church which could provide a properly catholic context to the parochial system.

Reflecting on experience

If the place where you live needed a new heating system:

- who would you ask for advice and what would be their qualifications;
- who would you ask to do the work and what would be their qualifications;
- what would be your own role and contribution?

What might this reflection say to the Church about:

- the personal and the professional;
- the local agenda and wider factors?

EXERCISE

📖 **Read Acts 3:11–16.** Religious experience can easily become the source of deep division and polarisation. Consider the following points:

- Peter owns kinship with those who hold very different views. Different contexts and opinions have a deeper commonness;

▶▶

- Peter denies any power in himself. Any authority he exercises is a gift from God;
- deeply religious people may be those most likely to 'kill the one who leads to life';
- faith in Jesus is foundational: the work and witness of the Church stems from this base;
- this is a message for all who will hear it;
- the clue is to recognise what is 'holy and good' and accept it.

William Laud (1573–1648)

William Laud was born in Reading and became successively scholar, fellow and then President of St John's College, Oxford. In 1622 he was involved in a famous debate with a Jesuit called Fisher, held before the king, Prince Charles and their courtiers. The mother of the royal favourite, the Duke of Buckingham, was contemplating conversion to Roman Catholicism. Laud was asked to debate with Fisher to make clear the position of the Church of England and to persuade this lady to remain an Anglican. In fact she eventually joined the Roman Catholic Church, but a book was published giving an account of the debate and it stands as a classical statement of how Laud articulated Anglicanism in the seventeenth century.

His basic contention was that the existence of the Orthodox Communion was a huge contradiction of any claims Rome might make to be the universal Church. Moreover, he reiterated Hooker's argument that the Church of England was loyal to the doctrine and discipline of the early, undivided Church and thus stood as the proper manifestation of the catholic Church in Britain.

In an interesting section, Laud acknowledges the need for official ministers of the Church to be particularly loyal to her doctrine – especially the canons and *The Book of Common Prayer*. This links to a 'Declaration' (for which he was responsible in 1628) attached to the Thirty-Nine Articles, which stated that there should be silence on points of controversy. Laud believed that faith is held by the Church as a corporation. Individuals could explore the nature of faith and its appropriate expression but in public there should be loyalty to the corporate faith of the Church. It was important to have mechanisms for testing, refining and recasting the public expression of faith, but such explorations needed to be ordered and dignified, not subject to individual or local particularities. Thus controversy about the Thirty-Nine Articles was not for public debate. This could only be harmful; explorations needed to be conducted in ways that did not undermine confidence in the Church's public proclamation. He also insisted that the words of the key documents had to be accepted in their plain sense.

By 1633 Laud had become Archbishop of Canterbury, having been successively Bishop of St Davids, Bath and Wells, and London. Now he was a key adviser to King Charles I. As the royal government became increasingly unpopular, Laud suffered a similar fate. He was well-known as one of the Crown's chief officers, particularly as a member of the judicial bodies that meted out harsh punishment to puritan dissidents like William Prynne, who had his ears cut off. Laud was strongly concerned to uphold order and to quell those who disturbed it, since he believed that Church and State had God-given roles in establishing appropriate ways of organising ordinary life. As a person of his time, he accepted and utilised the brutal methods of trying to take this commission seriously.

By 1640 the government had become very unpopular as England moved towards the outbreak of civil war. Laud was impeached by the Long Parliament and spent three years in prison. Then in 1644, when the war was raging, he was accused of treason. In 1645 a Bill of Attainder was passed, declaring him guilty without a trial. When the House of Lords voted for this Bill there were only fourteen peers present. It was passed on the same day that *The Book of Common Prayer* was abolished in favour of a *Directory of Public Worship*. On 10 January 1645, Laud was executed at Tower Hill, asserting his loyalty to the Church of England.

EXERCISE

Should the official ministers of the Church be especially loyal to her doctrine?

Is public argument in bodies like synods a damaging witness to the order and oneness of God? What are the alternatives?

Is the faith primarily held by the Church as a corporation, within which individuals find a place, or does the faith of individuals make up the Church?

The case for a national Church: beyond parochialism

Laud offers a substantial development of the theology of Richard Hooker. The latter had tried to help the Church of England clarify an identity against outside forces – whether Roman Catholic or radical Protestant. In the seventeenth century the Church of England was more secure against Rome and continental Protestantism, not least due to the unifying effect of *The Book of Common Prayer* and the political success of Elizabeth I. In Laud's time the danger came from the threat of dissolution from within.

In the previous century England had thrown off the Roman dictatorship of papal supremacy. Now, in Laud's time, there was a movement to overthrow the dictatorship of the Tudor kings. This was part of a movement from below, as citizens discovered their own sense of identity and flexed their muscles over against the monarchy and the traditional trappings of establishment. Laud stood against this popular, and ultimately Protestant, trend by asserting the importance of there being some official power 'from above', a God-given authority to help order and rule both Church and State. In his own time he was not understood, since he was so clearly identified with the monarchical despotism of the Tudors. Yet in his writings we can discern a plea for recognising the wisdom of the centre ground. This plea remained unheard amidst the gathering momentum that issued in the clash of civil war between the theologies of Catholicism and Protestantism.

Key principles

Laud's basic theme is that of unity and order. He lived in an age of developing division and conflict: Church against State, King against Parliament, Anglican against puritan, authority against freedom. Amidst all these divisions he wanted unity and order. He desired to reconcile what seemed to be contrary and incompatible. Local distinctions required a common foundation. The Church is one, holy, catholic and apostolic. Rome had forfeited her role as focus of this unity – but like other Anglicans Laud understood the deeper challenge of such a necessity.

The one and the many

His theological approach was influenced by Thomas Aquinas and the tradition of Aristotle, thus linking him with much of the medieval Catholic Church, despite his strong opposition to Rome. Aquinas had influenced Hooker, and Laud builds upon this foundation with great skill.

It is not easy today to understand Laud's way of thinking, because in a democratic culture modern minds understand the world in mechanistic terms as a collection of individual parts, each with its own identity and rights, needing to be formed into a harmonious whole. This task requires negotiation, management and contract so as to safeguard individual rights while creating a workable whole. Hence ours is an age of citizen's charters and personal rights. We begin with the apparent reality of the many and seek to construct an acceptable oneness or harmony. This task depends upon human ingenuity and never manages to succeed.

To Laud the universal society was not like a machine where the parts have to be ordered in such a way that they can work together and be one. Rather, society was more like a body: not an 'organisation' but an 'organism'. There was no notion of individual rights; the key concept was rather that of duty to the whole. Everything exists only as part of a whole. The body comes first and is primary, the individual is secondary and subsequent. The one is the prime reality, everything else exists only as a constituent part of this whole. Yet oneness for Laud is located in the will of the creator God, whose particular purpose for each unique part of creation is designed to ensure the harmony of the body or organism that is human being. Hence the importance of discerning and upholding the proper order for the various parts of creation, so that the unity for which we have been created can be more fully realised, not by our construction but by our discovery of God's will and purpose.

The essence of creation is that God imposes order on primeval chaos, putting it into a particular shape within which its life forces can be properly developed. The Book of Genesis recounts the creation of a multitude of different parts, that are given an order which provides harmony. Human beings are tempted to upset this order; the way to restoration is not through human construct, but through discernment of God's will and way in the hierarchy of being.

EXERCISE

What are the key differences between an organisation and an organism in terms of Church structures?

How does Laud's theology relate to your reflection on installing a new heating system?

Potential and purpose

This notion is made clearer by Aristotle's distinction between matter and form. This may seem rather technical but it is essential in understanding Laud's approach to theology. 'Matter' here basically means the 'stuff out of which things are made'. (It does not simply mean material as in 'that chair is made of matter'.) The term labels the potential of a particular thing to become what it has been created to be. 'Form', however, is used to signify the shape that the potential should take in order to fulfil its proper purpose. Thus, for example, each person is created as matter with the potential to become something; the proper 'form' for each person is the correct shape through which such potential should develop. In this way both 'matter' and 'form' are dynamic: matter is something that is going to grow and develop, its form will be the shape through which that growth and development take place. This is important because today we assume 'matter' and 'form' signify something static. 'Form' is not a fixed mould but the changing shape through which matter develops its potential. Hooker's idea of laws presupposes this kind of thinking.

God is the only being who stands outside this understanding of matter and form; everything else is created by God as matter-with-potential and with a form, a God-given path that it should travel. In this sense every part of creation is important and has a particular contribution to make to the working of the whole. Every part has a dynamic, which is related to the dynamic of other parts, for the purposes of the whole to be realised. This is a recipe for continuing development and change, to fulfil an order that will hold all things in harmony and unity.

If any part tries to realise its potential in a way that is not within its proper or appropriate form, this will undermine its own development and the harmonious working of the whole. The many find their meaning and fulfilment only in terms of the one.

EXERCISE
📖 **Read 1 Corinthians 12.**

Assess how Paul's teaching relates to that of Aristotle.

A given vocation

When Laud applied this way of thinking to his own society, it explained the problems of disorder and dis-ease. For example, the puritans were stirring up revolt against the divinely appointed monarch and trying to guide national life into a form for which it was not intended. The result was disorder. This kind of misguided development would destroy society and prevent it realising its proper potential ('matter') because some of the parts were developing in inappropriate ways ('forms'). Hence Laud's fanatical concern that order and unity be defended and imposed by those commissioned to fulfil this particular task.

Government and Church must both face the challenge of discovering and developing the appropriate forms of order and harmony that God wills for the whole of society, just as each individual must discover his or her particular vocation to contribute to the well-being of this divine order. There is no concept here of personal freedom in the modern sense of individual liberty or self-determination; the freedom of each individual in this context is the freedom to choose to become the 'form' each is supposed to be.

Thus any one who breaks the required order, either as an individual or as a corporation, as a government or as a monarch, by failing to discern and fulfil their God-given potential, will fall from their allotted course and incur the following serious consequences:
• offence against God, who created that particular part with its own matter and form;
• offence against the other parts, that is fellow men and women;
• offence against the harmony and order of the whole, as intended by God;
• offence against the self, because that part is no longer true to what it has been created to be.

The result is spiritual suicide. For Laud, the forms of order and unity necessary for the public welfare were being broken up into smaller, unconnected, essentially rival and private interests. Each group or individual simply wanted their will to prevail, whatever the cost to the whole.

This task of discovery and development is hard work. It requires discernment, trust in a greater power and purpose than can be immediately perceived, and a willingness to live with change and uncertainty. It is a *theological* task because all discernment is to do with the will of God and the gift of life from God.

Tradition

Laud appealed to tradition and to antiquity. He was well-read in the Fathers and quotes extensively from them. But he recognised, as Hooker had, that there might be some overriding need that demands a shift beyond tradition and that this is acceptable because the form is expected to develop and to change. Thus tradition is not something static, like a rigid mould that restricts any new kind of development. The form will change with the potentiality of the matter. Tradition is crucial, and provides clues about what the shape might be, but it should not be determinative in the narrow sense of closing down possibilities. Tradition is important, then, but it is not narrowly prescriptive. Hooker had a similar understanding of tradition, allowing that it could change but that any development had to be related to what had been given before. There had to be an important measure of consistency.

EXERCISE

What would be the result of your asking yourself (or your church):

• what is the potential that I am (we are) called to fulfil;
• what are the appropriate forms in which that potentiality might be properly expressed at this time;
• how can I (we) be confident that these judgements are true?

Theological method: an Anglican middle way

Laud's key emphasis is that truth usually lies between two extremes. He felt that the Church of England was unfairly criticised by both papists and puritans. He wrote:

> She professes the ancient catholic faith but the Romanists condemn her because of novelty in her doctrine. She practises Church government as it has always been in all ages and in all places where the Church of Christ has taken root ever since the apostles' time, but the separatists blame her for anti-Christian forms of government. The plain truth is the Church of England is between these two factions as between two millstones . . . Unless your majesty look to it, to whose trust she is committed, she will be ground to powder by these two. (Laud, 1847–1860, Vol. II, p. xiii)

The middle way is difficult. The truth usually lies between the two extremes and is to be upheld by those divinely called to that task. Further, Laud insisted that Christianity had always been an attempt to

balance two extremes and then reconcile beliefs which on the surface
are contradictory. These extremes included:

- transcendence and immanence, God is over all yet present in the particular;
- word and sacrament;
- faith and works;
- freedom and law;
- revelation and reason.

At one level, there can seem to be real incompatibilities between these
pairs but at a deeper level there can be harmony and truth. For Laud, the
contradiction between apparently irreconcilable positions is often
caused by the limitations of the human perspective. In God's purpose
and process there may well be oneness. For this reason he is keen to
acknowledge the fallibility of Christians and of Churches, and to recognise the need to be open to change. He wrote:

> The scripture where it is plain should guide the Church. The Church,
> where there is doubt or difficulty should expand the scripture. Yet
> as neither the scripture should be forced nor the Church so bound
> up as upon just and further evidence the Church may revise that
> which in any case has slipped by her. (Laud, 1847–1860, Vol. II,
> p. xv)

The notion of 'further evidence' and of the fallibility of the Church is
crucial but complex. It would have been more straightforward for Laud
to adopt the approach of his critics and award absolute authority to the
Church or to Scripture, gaining clarity, shelter and security. But he
believed that the potentiality given by God was living and developing,
and would take forms touched with newness as well as by tradition.
There would be 'further evidence' to challenge and sometimes to change
the form in which Christianity was called to be expressed, not least since
human freedom invited the possibility of error although God will
always give resources for those who choose to use them to correct their
errors. For this reason humility was essential, since not all questions
have been infallibly settled. Moreover, the human intellect had limitations. No one could know the whole truth.

Re-formation

Therefore re-formation will be part of the Christian journey: as potentiality develops, there will be a re-forming of the ways in which it is

expressed and shared. Laud identifies five ingredients necessary to make re-formation.

1. **Humility:** so as to recognise errors, to accept further evidence and to allow the interpretation of Scripture and tradition to grow and change.

2. **The courage to change:** Potentiality is always moving and pushing forms to re-form. For human beings, there is a strong instinct to resist change because we feel secure with what we think we know. A living God always has much more to teach us and thus our 'forms' for knowing must be receptive to newness, otherwise they become idols. Change requires courage.

3. **Unity and order is never static:** but a quality which embraces the growth and development of potential. Unity and order provides a shape not a strait-jacket at a particular time.

4. **Theology must be a developmental discipline:** using the method of Scripture, tradition and further evidence. These ingredients must be in a dynamic relationship.

5. **Truth is primary:** Unity is desirable but truth is even more important. In the process of trying to realise potential in a way that contributes to the order and harmony of the whole, there will always be provisionality, since human perceptions are fallible and limited. The 'forms' for unity will be penultimate. Yet the unity God wills in creation is ultimate and our faith in the truth of unity and order is more important than any form it might seem to take at a particular time. The human view will always be partial but faith can trust in a deeper, fuller, more complete unity, providing a vision and a call to move ever beyond any expression of unity we might be achieving, towards something more profound. Thus truth is primary but attempts to realise it will always be secondary and 'in process'.

EXERCISE

'The truth usually lies between two extremes.' Can you think of examples?

'Further evidence will lead to re-formation.' What are the dangers in this theology?

The Anglican commission: a national Church

The Church of England was commissioned to give focus to parochial Churches and should root this responsibility in four fundamentals: Scripture as the rule of faith, the sacraments, the creeds and episcopacy (the authority of bishops and the diocese as the key unit of the Church, with dioceses being joined through episcopal collegiality).

These 'fundamentals', highlighted by Laud in the 1530s, correspond to those acknowledged at the Lambeth Conference of Anglican Bishops in 1888. They were seen to be essential ingredients to the shape of any 'form' that Christianity might grow into, and to be determinative measures of 'appropriateness' in the development of the potential. Around these fundamentals Churches will add details with regard to matters such as liturgy and order, but such ways of expressing the faith will be 'things indifferent'. This does not mean that they are unimportant but that they are features which will grow and develop in different places and in different times.

Areas of responsibility for the national Church

Scripture

Laud recognised Scripture as the word of God but, like Hooker, he realised the need for interpretation. And those who interpret Scripture are not infallible. He wrote, 'The papists believe in an infallible church, and the puritans believe in an infallible Bible.' For Laud, the Bible is the word of God because the Church teaches this truth and Scripture gives this testimony in itself. The Holy Spirit makes Scripture the word of God and natural reason can connect with Scripture as the word of God. All these forces interact and from such interaction can come what he calls 'further evidence'.

Scripture is the living word, which does not close down possibilities. Rather, it feeds and nourishes the potentialities of God's creatures to enable us to develop more appropriately through the process of re-formation. At the heart of Christianity is the crucifixion, the supreme sign of re-formation as potentiality is called to its fullest completion. Scripture is a living word that affirms and invites this challenging process. It does not provide neat formulas and structures within which Christians can be safe and static. This dynamism of Scripture requires a larger context than the purely local.

Authority

The fundamental issue in the seventeenth century was the question of authority: in relation to the interpretation of Scripture, the power of the Church and her leaders, and the role of monarchy and government. Catholicism looked to papal lordship; puritans held to the supremacy of Scripture when interpreted by the elect.

Laud tried to find a way between these two extremes and argued that there should be three foci of authority, with each responsible for making appropriate order together.

- *The Crown*, of which he wrote, 'the monarch becomes an ecclesiastical person through the act of coronation' (Laud, 1847–1860, Vol. VI, p. 245). Thus the monarch exercised authority in the Church not as a lay person, but as an ecclesiastical person.
- *Convocation*, the college of clergy and bishops.
- *Parliament*, which in Laud's time represented the laity.

Each of these three elements is involved in the exercise of authority. However, decisions about worship and doctrine are to be made by those best qualified – which meant the Crown and the Convocation, the ecclesiastical persons. Laud stressed the danger of fanatical amateurs who would end decency, order and unity.

This links with the point made in the previous chapter about Hooker's stressing that 'reason' was not a universal faculty but a gift to some people for a particular purpose. Hooker had an aristocratic view of authority. Laud similarly pointed to the danger of fanatical amateurs. He insisted that 'Churchmen and none but Churchmen' must do public work, 'according to their calling and their warrant'. He writes (using the exclusive language that here and elsewhere reflects the period):

> Yet I hope Churchmen will never be so proud but that if any lay, religious man, with larger comprehension than themselves will offer in private any help to them, they would lend an open ear to it and after, with prudent consideration, do what is fit. (Laud, 1847–1860, Vol. VI, p. 97)

Potentiality and form must be realised. Many parts will have contributions to make, but God commissions some to be responsible for public order and unity. Those with this warrant and commission must listen to others and act when they think it is prudent, but all must be done with decency so as to preserve that essential witness to the unity and oneness of God and of God's will.

Thus further evidence can come from all kinds of sources, not just those officially appointed to consider and weigh it. Yet there will be control. The alternative is the scenario Laud saw developing in his own time, when order and oneness was destroyed in the cause of factional interest and the desires of fanatical, self-appointed amateurs. Beneath the surface of public order and unity much can be explored and debated, but once this essential framework is ignored both the parts and the whole will suffer.

Worship

Laud applies the same ideas to worship and stresses the importance of a uniform structure. There may be some who can dispense with such things, but he argues that the great majority of people value order and structure in worship. The puritans at that time wanted a much freer approach to worship than *The Book of Common Prayer* allowed. Laud recognised that 'the inner worship of the heart is the great service of God, and no service is acceptable without it' (Laud, 1847–1860, Vol. II, p. xi).

But he goes on to argue that humankind is a physical as well as a spiritual being: all knowledge comes through the gateway of the senses, which need to be ordered and structured. If there is too much informality and individuality then the witness to God's greater order and unity will be destroyed. Worship witnesses to the oneness of God, and to our oneness in God, not to the variety of human tastes and aspiration which are penultimate and secondary to the deeper truth of God as one. God is the God of order, beauty and harmony. These things are essential ingredients of the form of public worship. The truth normally lies between two extremes and is focused in God's deeper oneness. Thus, for Laud, Anglican unity is established and expressed in the order of worship, as set out in *The Book of Common Prayer*. 'Unity cannot long continue in the Church when uniformity is shut out at the Church door' (Laud, 1847–1860, Vol. IV, p. 60).

Unity

Four things are necessary if unity is to be discovered and developed. First, theological argument must be left to the theologians. As with Hooker, those inspired by God's gift of reason are the people to pursue theological debate, though they should be open to insights from others. Parts have particular functions here, a view that stands opposed to the modern tendency to pretend that each person has the right to comment about anything! Second, Laud adds that theologians should investigate differences in a spirit of charity, acknowledging the truth of unity even when human efforts to express it are flawed. Third, the fundamentals of Scripture, sacraments, creeds and episcopacy remain essential. Fourth, Christians must join together in common worship. Whatever the views or aspirations of particular individuals and groups it is vital to join together in common worship, because 'eventually you will receive unity of the spirit' (Bourne, 1947, p. 156). The key word is 'eventually'. Unity is the gift of the Spirit of God, not a human construct, and all Christians should observe the discipline of common public worship so that together they can wait on this gift, which is beyond our own making. 'Eventually' the God-given potentiality of all the parts will discover a unity of spirit, even though ways of wishing to express this will inevitably continue to differ.

To utilise these four ingredients for unity most effectively, Christians should cultivate what Laud calls 'habit', particularly the discipline and humility of joining together in public worship, as vital to the development of the multitude of potentialities that make up human society. While acknowledging the importance of private exploration, discussion and debate, the priority of oneness is owned as being in God.

Conclusion: the Laudian approach

For Anglicanism, Laud based his approach upon the conviction that the truth will lie between two extremes. To discern and follow truth there needs to be balance, together with the given framework provided by the four fundamentals of Scripture, sacraments, creed and episcopacy. It is also important that we recognise that:

- within that framework private judgement has a place, for individuals have a potentiality and a contribution to make. This contribution should be made within a structure of witnessing to the public unity focused in common worship;
- the Church has no claim to infallibility;
- the Church will value its tradition but not blindly;
- the Church will be open to new light, what he calls 'further evidence';
- worship has the key role, through the ministry of word and sacrament, in the public witness to unity and order;
- all should come and be part of public worship. Order is essential in worship, but many people have a contribution to make;
- this wholeness, coming from many contributions, is rooted in the

discipline and order of the threefold ministry – an aristocracy of authority;

Laud's theology is essentially occasional and not systematic. It was developed in various arguments and battles. Laud writes in one of his papers that this is the form of Scripture: it is also occasional. The dilemma is not just finding this way between extremes, it is actually about the danger of being ground between the two extremes because we tend to seek a 'way' rather than the truth. The way for one individual or group might lie more towards one extreme than the other but the truth would always be of a deeper order and unity. The crucial ingredient, according to Laud, is humility.

So Laud argues for public order, unity and loyalty, focused in the 'habit' of common worship; room for private debate and exploration; the reality of 'further evidence' leading to change and re-forming, as proper potential is developed; and the oversight and control of these three factors by those called and commissioned to this task, though they too may need to be subject to private correction and teaching from others.

EXERCISE

What do you think are the advantages and the problems that this way of thinking might bring in the contemporary Church? Could there be 'structures of organisation' to allow such forces to operate? How do Laud's views relate to the modern 'democratic' way of thinking?

How do you evaluate Laud's different conditions for re-formation: humility before the possibility of error and of further evidence; courage to change, to re-form; the dynamic of order and unity; theology as a developmental discipline; and truth as primary and prior, given by God not created by us?

You might reflect further whether Laud's recipe for unity can help us today.

In particular, you might wonder which of his 'ingredients' will lead 'eventually' to the unity of the Spirit: leaving theological argument to the theologians; holding fast to the four fundamentals (Scripture, sacraments, creed, episcopacy); joining together in common worship?

EXERCISE

📖 **Read Acts 3:17–26.** How does this text relate to the arguments advanced by Laud about Church order and systems of authority? You may like to consider the following points:

- the reality of ignorance, in the people and in their leaders, and the need for 'further evidence';
- Scripture as containing the key clues, though they are not easily recognisable by everyone;
- repentance and forgiveness as foundational to the Christian journey and re-formation as a basic process;
- obedience to Christ: oneness is given in him, not created by us;
- God appointing and commissioning prophets to herald and interpret this good news;
- a Gospel for 'all the people on earth', not just for the gathered few; the Church as an organism not an organisation;
- in Christ we are blessed; through worship we are given oneness, our part is repentance and humility.

Further reading

Avis, P (1989), *Anglicanism and the Christian Church*, Edinburgh, T and T Clark.

Bourne, E C E (1947), *The Anglicanism of William Laud*, London, SPCK.

Carlton, C (1987), *Archbishop William Laud*, London, Routledge and Kegan Paul.

Collins, W E (ed.) (1895), *Archbishop Laud Commemorated*, London, A Southey and Company.

Evans, G R (1990), *Authority in the Church*, Norwich, Canterbury Press.

Green, I (1994), Anglicanism in Stuart and Hanoverian England, in S Gilley and W J Sheils (eds), *A History of Religion in Britain*, chapter 9, Oxford, Blackwell.

Laud, W (1639), *A Relation of the Conference Between William Laud and Mr Fisher*, London, Richard Badger.

More, P E and Cross, F L (1935), *Anglicanism*, London, SPCK.

5. SHAPING A SPIRITUALITY

Introduction

After the struggles of civil war and the accompanying explosion of religious freedom, the Church of England was re-established in a form that recognised the importance of Laud's approach to order, authority and a way between two extremes. The revised structures needed an infusion of new life and this is best illustrated by William Law, whose teaching and example provided the seedbed of the great revivals in the nineteenth-century Church of England – both evangelical and catholic. These movements recognised that, in an increasingly challenging culture for the Anglican tradition, each Christian needed an ever deeper sense of her or his own vocation and discipline, as a key ingredient in the outworking of a wider parochial system.

Reflecting on experience
How does your own experience of prayer relate to the public worship and witness of the Church?

EXERCISE
📖 **Read Acts 4:1–22.** There are two systems of spirituality in this encounter:
- the system of temple and high priesthood, with established teachers, leaders, elders and a formal syllabus of education;
- the system of empowerment of individuals of no formal education by the resurrection of Jesus Christ from the dead, and the gift of the Holy Spirit. ▶▶

How do these systems relate to each other:
- from the perspective of the Jewish leaders;
- from the perspective of Peter and John;
- from the perspective of 'the people';
- from the perspective of the man who had been healed?

William Law (1686–1761)

Law was born at Kings Cliffe near Peterborough in Northamptonshire and educated at Emmanuel College, Cambridge. In 1711 he was ordained deacon but he was not priested for a number of years afterwards. He was elected to a fellowship in his college and seemed set for a traditional academic career. However, he was a nonjuror, believing that the Stuarts were by divine right the legitimate monarchs of England and therefore refusing to take the oath of allegiance to William and Mary, and later to the Hanoverians. Law was a faithful member of the Church of England but he was unable to accept public office because of this unwillingness to swear an oath of allegiance to the current monarch. There is no subsequent record of him practising as a minister. In 1714 he resigned his fellowship and for the rest of his life he worked as a tutor and private chaplain.

Law first came to notice in 1717 when he published a series of letters in reply to a book by Bishop Hoadly of Bangor. The bishop argued for a reasonable Christianity, earthed in sincerity and integrity. Law's letter of reply indicates something of the book's weaknesses and also of Law's own views: 'You will have left us neither priests nor sacraments nor church. And what has your Lordship given up in the ruin of these advantages? Why, only sincerity. This is the great universal atonement for all' (Inge, 1905, p. 129).

Law is clear that any individual struggle for integrity needs feeding by, and must be in relation to, a ministry, sacraments and Church. Christianity cannot be reduced to a matter of the individual standing before God. It has to be in a much larger context. This relates to Herbert's emphasis upon the essentially corporate nature of spirituality. It is important to note that Law starts with this emphasis because, while taking the centrality of the corporate for granted (in contrast to Herbert), much of his subsequent work places great emphasis upon a personal response to the Gospel.

In 1726 he published a book called *Christian Perfection* emphasising the grace of God which is poured out to give hope to humankind. He writes there, 'Revelation has dispersed all the anxiety of man's vain conjecture. It has brought him acquainted with God, and by adding heaven to earth' (Stranks, 1961, p. 177). For Law, the revelation of God in Jesus Christ has added heaven to earth, eternity to time. It has opened up such a glorious view of things that even in its present condition humanity can be filled with that peace which passes all understanding. The Christ is a sign of hopefulness and confidence which makes sense of human aspirations and of human weakness and failings. This confidence is what he calls 'Christian perfection' and it is focused in the person of Christ, the agent of the gift of God's grace.

EXERCISE

What do you think of Law's teaching about Christian perfection, especially the notion of adding heaven to earth?

'A Serious Call'

In 1729 Law wrote one of his most significant works, *A Serious Call to a Devout and Holy Life*. The title is characteristic of the author and of his views. His aim was to speak to his contemporaries, especially those who apparently conformed to religious observance. He lived in a time when there was an increasing recognition of the paradox that, although Christianity seemed firmly established in English life, there was in fact widespread cynicism and unbelief. Law believed that Christianity should have a clearly recognised identity, founded not upon an easy coherence with contemporary culture but upon a costly distinctiveness that could challenge and call others to a 'new' and more appropriate life within creation. This call started with the individual, but required a local structure for its nourishment and to enable an effective witness to be made.

For Law this distinctiveness is founded upon personal experience of knowing God: the life of prayer, recognising the grace and love of God, acknowledging the seriousness of each human life under God (the importance for each individual of the choices that this life involves), supporting the witnessing community and caring for the poor and needy.

> **EXERCISE**
> If *all* creation is involved in fulfilling God-given potential, in what
> ways are Christians called to be distinctive? Are Law's marks of
> Christian distinctiveness adequate?

The path of Christian distinctiveness

In *A Serious Call*, the technique which Law uses to explore the path of
Christian distinctiveness is to offer a series of character sketches, each of
which uses exaggeration so that the readers may more easily identify
what attracts or repels them, thus highlighting the key issue of individual
choice.

The life of prayer

The importance of personal prayer is illustrated by the story of Oura-
nius. He is a parson, a person of public prayer, who is transformed by
his own prayer life. 'When he first entered holy orders he had a great
contempt for all foolish and unreasonable people . . . but he has prayed
this spirit away' (Law, 1978, p. 303). Law continues:

> When he first came to his little village it was as disagreeable to him as
> a prison, and every day seemed too tedious to be endured in so retired
> a place. His parish was full of poor and mean people that were none
> of them fit for the conversation of a gentleman. He kept much at
> home, writ notes upon Homer, and sometimes thought it hard to be
> called to pray by any poor body when he was just in the midst of one
> of Homer's battles. But now his days are so far from being tedious or
> his parish too great a retirement, that he wants only more time to do
> that variety of good which his soul thirsts after. He now thinks the
> poorest creature in the parish good enough and great enough to
> deserve the humblest attendance, the kindest friendship, the tenderest
> office, he can possibly show. He is so far from wanting agreeable com-
> pany that he thinks there is no better conversation in the world than
> to be talking with poor and mean people about the Kingdom of God.
> He loves every soul in the parish as he loves himself because he prays
> for them as he prays for himself. (Law, 1978, p. 304)

Here is an example of the power of prayer to change a particular person. Despite the caricature characters, the change is not effected by the

parson's contact with the people (which would be our modern way of interpreting his transformation). In terms of the human effect of contact with his parishioners and the growth of respect and intimacy, Law is not expressing anything so 'natural'. He is clear that the change has come about because of the parson's *praying*. He prays for his parishioners as he prays for himself, and in this discipline of praying – of aiming heavenward for a more perfect and complete witnessing of God's grace and God's love – he recognises his shortcomings and his failures, and he is changed by a greater power so that all become precious and agreeable.

Prayer is not reflection which 'catches up' with the unfolding of life like a reactive discipline, rather prayer is putting oneself under God's power to better emulate the Christ of the gospels and so to be transformed in a way that makes us proactive agents of grace – taking love to others rather than seeing if any such thing can simply grow. Prayer changes people, who then are sent to change the world. It is proactive and powerful, not simply reactive and reflective. Even those who are rooted in public prayer need a discipline to wrestle with their own personal vocation.

EXERCISE

'Prayer is not a reflection which "catches" up with the unfolding of life . . . it is putting oneself under the power of God and so to be transformed.' How does this approach to prayer compare with that of George Herbert?

Recognising the grace and love of God

The perspective of the Christian journey is about being 'heavenward'. Each of us is given a vocation on earth and the spiritual task is to discern this vocation as something heavenward, that is in terms of God's call to a fuller and further life. This requires diligence now and a looking beyond the present.

Law illustrates this point by reference to another character, Octavius. He is an old scholar, much respected in the community, and getting very weak. Recognising that he is failing, Octavius devoted all his energy to devising a scheme to get a good stock of wine from the tavern, so that when he is no longer able to make the journey he might still enjoy a good drink. While he is busy organising this project, however, he dies, alone and comfortless, cut off from his creator (see Law, 1978, p. 177). Law uses this story to consider the reality of human mortality and the fact that in this penultimate life our aim should not be to redouble our efforts to preserve ourselves on earth, but rather to learn to live heavenward. This is the ultimate, and the real, focus of prayer. Octavius would have died much more richly in tune with his creator, and possibly not so prematurely, if he had not expended so much effort trying to get his present life just right and had the discipline to reach higher. Law was not minimising the value and importance of having a good cellar, but rather the fact that Octavius put *all* his energies into this project and thus lacked the discipline and rhythm of life which might have helped him put his endeavors more clearly within God's greater context. We tend to become obsessed with what is in fact penultimate, though ostensibly for our own benefit, and this undermines our spiritual life and cuts us off from our creator. Octavius looked down to his cellar, not up to heaven.

EXERCISE
How can Christians better witness to a sense of proportion in regard to the appropriate priorities in this life, and what are appropriate priorities for being 'heavenward'?

The seriousness of this life and its choices

The serious choices which constitute human life are illustrated by a sketch of two sisters, each living independently on an annual income of £200 (not an inconsiderable amount of money in the eighteenth century). One was called Flavia (which means 'extravagant'). She is selfish and worldly. She lives in London in the fashionable world and spends her time going to plays, the opera and parties. But if anybody catches her in the right mood she will give them half a crown and encourage others to be charitable. Law writes:

> Flavia would be a miracle of piety if she was but half as careful with her soul as she is with her body. The rising of a pimple on her face, the sting of a gnat, would make her keep to her room for two or three days. And she thinks they are very rash people who do not take care of things in time. She will sometimes read a book of piety if it is a short one, if it is much commended for its style and language and she can know where to borrow it! (Law, 1978, p. 107)

This is clearly a caricature of a person of fashion, but an uncomfortably familiar picture of the spiritual life.

Flavia is compared with her sister Miranda (which means 'wonderful'). Law recognises that human life is about choices and he gives clear indications of his own preferences! Miranda wants to put everything to right and reasonable use: 'excepting her victuals she never spends £10 a year on herself' (Law, 1978, p. 114). She prays 'early and late', she regularly reads the New Testament and she makes clothes for the needy. More challenging, she is generous to the wicked, as one of the best ways of reclaiming them. This is the great Gospel insight that people are changed by love: not by being judged and punished, but by being offered generosity and affirmation. Miranda justifies being generous, including to the wicked:

> Shall I withhold a little money or food from my fellow creature for fear he shall not be good enough to receive it of me? Do I beg God to deal with me, not according to my merit but according to his own great goodness, and shall I be so absorbed as to withhold my charity from a poor brother because he may not deserve it? (Law, 1978, p. 118)

She says that the New Testament demands indiscriminate charity. This is something for our prayers, since such generosity does not come naturally to us, and praying can often be a way of judging others and simply seeking God's generosity for ourselves.

Here is an issue right at the heart of the Christian life – it is not easy or natural to be generous to the wicked or to want to change people with love. This has to be worked at and the contrast between the two sisters calls for a stark choice about the ingredients and focus of Christian life. Miranda is simple, serious, holy, generous and unjudging: not naturally, but because of the struggle between herself and the Gospel – the practice of what we call *spirituality*. Miranda struggles to make this choice of renunciation, discipline and devotion to the way of Christ.

Her story also makes clear that, because of our human weakness, we need forms and a routine of daily prayer, to be a focus for our reflection on the New Testament, our daily lives and the challenge to be generous with what has been given to us, and to seek to change people by love. These qualities are not natural to us in our fallen state and we thus need discipline and structure.

EXERCISE

Consider the characters of Flavia and Miranda. What can we learn with regard to personal discipline and public witness?

The witnessing community

Law recognised that the Christian life was not easy for us on our own. To take the Gospel seriously we need the support of others; those who do so must 'unite themselves into little societies'. These little societies must profess voluntary poverty, profess virginity or chastity (which included faithfulness within marriage), express themselves through 'retirement' (by which he means humility and modesty), show devotion to Christ, 'live on the bare necessities' and 'relieve others by charity'.

Thus the life of prayer of the Christian community is expressed consistently in a practical way, especially measured by its relationship to those in need. Law recognised that such a 'little Christian community' would be a remnant within a parish. There will only be some Christians called to this serious and salt-like witness. Yet this witness must be made for the sake of the rest. This relates to the nature of Anglican tradition, in that the notion of 'parish' is a dynamic between the minority who seek to observe the disciplines of the spiritual life, in public and in private (such as Herbert and his household), and the rest of the community whose engagement with the Gospel in any formal sense will be occasional and partial.

Law himself practised this model in Kings Cliffe, where he returned to live in a small community with two single ladies, acting as their chaplain. He and his companions were faithful and loyal members of the parish church, yet conscientious in their own renunciation, discipline and devotion.

Those called to such a deep spiritual engagement need to recognise the importance of being with others in a small community, sometimes within the broader Christian congregation and certainly within the wider community. Law and his companions remained loyal members of the flock in Kings Cliffe, even though they set themselves a different way of witness. Law was clear that all of God's children are called towards a common standard of love and graciousness, but some have a particular vocation to model and advertise these things, not for their own glorification but by renunciation, discipline and a devotion to Christ that simply glorifies God.

EXERCISE

What might be the danger of establishing 'little societies' within the broader congregation?

How might a small, disciplined group become a necessary leaven within the wider community?

Caring for those in need

Calidus (which means 'cold') is a successful businessman who does not have much interest in anything except his work. He is always in a hurry, but occasionally he offers short prayers asking for God's help and blessing as he dashes about. However, he maintains one important discipline: 'to get out of town every Saturday, and keep the Sunday as a day of quiet and refreshment in the country' (Law, 1978, p. 80). Calidus is a decent, sound citizen. But his approach is, for Law, very cold-hearted, very self-centred. In fact it is the antithesis of proper Christianity. To Calidus, Christianity is a faith fitted around his busy life, offering short occasional prayers and keeping Sunday as a day to recharge himself so that he can go back into battle refreshed on Monday. This may be a useful regime of therapy and some kind of cry for help when it is needed, but for Law it is not the appropriate Christian life. If Calidus understood what it meant to be a Christian businessman then he would want to give time to consider how his work could glorify God.

Christians need discipline and frameworks. It is not enough simply to ride on the back of the great state religious machine or an apparently Christian culture. Moreover, if Calidus began to consider how his life as a Christian businessman could glorify God, this would involve exploration of how his time could be spent for the general good of humankind – rather than simply seeking refreshment for himself. Spirituality is the discipline which asks regularly, and in a serious way, 'Is my life appropriate to the values and insights of the Gospel of Jesus Christ?'

Law offers similar advice to the wealthy, arguing that nothing is more glorious than doing good, which makes us like God who is good. Thus there is no use of money that is so glorious as devoting it to works of love and mercy. When we have satisfied our own sober and reasonable wants, we must not store up things for ourselves but rather we must spend our resources on the needy. Law practised what he professed. In King's Cliffe the small community in which he lived had a joint income of £3000 per year, which was a very large amount of money. They lived on ten per cent and gave away the rest, an unusual interpretation of tithing! The local vicar frequently complained because of the vagabonds and tramps who flocked to the village to receive this generous charity. Law held that it was his duty to give and that if others sinned by misusing what he gave, he was not to judge them. If people came to him in need, he had to give. He was a steward of God's bounty: on the kitchen fire there was always a saucepan of broth, a pile of shirts was always ready by the door. A lady who read *A Serious Call* sent Law a cheque for £1000. He immediately invested it in a school for girls in the village. He performed what he believed the Gospel professed: look after your own basic needs, and then look in your community to see how you can offer signs to others of the bounty God has given.

The Christian life is the serious effort which goes beyond the occasional arrow prayer or keeping Sunday as a day of rest: it is an effort to reflect on life, on what we are given and on what we can give to those in need, according to the teaching and example of Jesus Christ and according to those principles of renunciation, discipline and devotion to Christ.

EXERCISE

How might we interpret Law's call for charity and generosity in terms of street beggars today?

Is a mix of occasional arrow prayers and a day of rest a more realistic style of Christian living for most people than Law's 'devout and holy life'? What answers does the Bible give to this question?

The place of public worship

Each individual is challenged to make choices about the disciplines of prayer and lifestyle. This can be aided by involvement in small societies of like-minded people, providing nourishment for their members and an example to others. But there is a key place for the wider Church, the parish and public worship. Law caused some consternation by his assertion that 'there is not one command in all the Gospel for public worship. And perhaps it is a duty that is least insisted upon in scripture of any other' (Law, 1978, pp. 50–51).

In fact he was not seeking to undermine the discipline of public worship; he and his companions were faithful attenders of the services in their parish church. Rather, Law was making the point that for many people public worship *becomes* their Christian life. Going to public worship can remove the challenge and discipline of needing a deeply spiritual life which wrestles with the particular choices each individual faces and the call to be heavenward. For Law, as for Herbert, public worship was an essential ingredient of the Christian life, but one which should focus and prompt the more personal choices each individual needs to make.

EXERCISE

What is the appropriate relationship between public worship and private prayer?

Revival in parish and national Church life

Law sowed seeds of Christian living and the seriousness of the spiritual engagement which were to be of enormous influence on both the evangelical and the catholic revivals of the eighteenth and nineteenth centuries. A number of prominent Christians stand in the tradition of William Law.

Methodism

John Wesley (1703–1791) developed class meetings to provide a structure for 'little societies' within which spiritual discipline and Christian learning could be nurtured – modelled on his own experience of forming a 'holy club' as a student. He was clear that this enterprise was to strengthen parochial life in the same way that Law had envisaged: attendance at public worship in the parish church was part of the required commitment.

Besides offering nurture to Church people, these small groups were ideal for welcoming and initiating others into the Christian life at a time when social changes were beginning to undermine any notion of an automatic connection between English culture and the established Church. Wesley further developed Law's approach by recognising that the 'little societies' required authorised leadership, with skills in teaching and in pastoral care.

Evangelical revival

Charles Simeon (1759–1836) spent over fifty years as vicar of Holy Trinity Church in Cambridge. He played a key role in the evangelical revival within the Church of England. Like Wesley he organised small groups to provide the opportunity for more personal engagement within the life of the local Church. He visited the various groups in turn. They had a number of different functions which included Bible study, prayer and co-ordinating visiting in every part of the parish.

Simeon recognised the importance of encouraging such opportunities for personal engagement at a wider level, to nourish the life of the national Church. Thus he began sermon classes to help train students who felt called to ministry and he offered opportunities for the study of doctrine in Cambridge. He was also instrumental in establishing overseas missions and in founding a body of trustees to secure and administer Church patronage according to principles that would ensure the continuation of an evangelical approach to ministry and Christian life at parish level. This became 'The Simeon Trustees'.

Like Wesley, Simeon placed a key emphasis upon the Bible as a primary resource – something that was implicit in Law. He valued *The Book of Common Prayer* and the discipline of public worship as the unifying force in the established Church.

Catholic revival

John Henry Newman (1801–1890) was a key leader of the Catholic Revival which became known as the Oxford Movement. He was an evangelical in his teens and in his subsequent career retained many of the emphases which Law had crystallised in regard to a serious personal spirituality within the framework of the parochial system. The movement arose from a small 'holy club' type of gathering and through their 'Tracts for the Times' issued an appeal for a deeper seriousness about the Christian life in an increasingly critical culture. For Tractarians, the parish organisation was based upon the principles of 'little societies' to provide a more engaging environment for a variety of activities and pastoral responsibilities.

Like Simeon, the Tractarians were concerned about the appropriate revival of the national Church, with a special emphasis upon scholarship and teaching. They held that the main key resource required for the times lay in rediscovering the insights and emphases of Church tradition, particularly the Fathers and the Anglican divines.

EXERCISE

What might be the appropriate marks of personal seriousness for Christians today?

Does the structure of 'little societies' help or hinder the proper flowering of individual potential, and the effective functioning of a parish?

Law emphasised personal disciplines and choices. Evangelicals underlined the importance of Scripture; catholics underlined the importance of tradition. How can these three elements best relate to one another and to the life of the local church?

In order to revive and nourish the national Church:
- Simeon established societies of like-minded people (for example the Church Missionary Society, Trustees for patronage);
- Newman and the Tractarians looked to the appointed leadership of the Church (bishops and clergy);
- Wesley began a movement towards forming an alternative structure.

EXERCISE

How would you evaluate these three different approaches to Church renewal?

📖 **Read Acts 4:23–37.** How might this text relate to William Law's account of personal piety and parochial systems, and its development in the evangelical and catholic revivals? You may like to consider:
- the dynamic between the wider community and the committed 'believers';
- the 'believers' joined together in prayer to God;
- finding guidance and reassurance in words of Scripture;
- the Gospel message healing differences between the 'believers' and others;
- believers as a distinctive group within the wider community.

This last point may be developed. The distinctiveness of believers results from a number of features of their lifestyle and spirituality. These include their oneness in heart and mind (the example of, and invitation to, unity); their sharing of material goods; their witness to the resurrection of Jesus; their attention to human needs; their use of resources for charitable rather than ecclesiastical purposes; and their recognition of the authority of the apostles. How important are these different elements in your view?

Further reading

Chadwick, O (1983), *Newman*, Oxford, Oxford University Press.

Chadwick, O (1970), *The Victorian Church*, two volumes, London, A and C Black.

Hopkins, H E (1977), *Charles Simeon of Cambridge*, London, Hodder and Stoughton.

Hylson-Smith, K (1988), *Evangelicals in the Church of England, 1734–1984*, Edinburgh, T and T Clark.

Law, W (1978), *A Serious Call to a Devout and Holy Life*, New York, Paulist Press.

Moorman, J R H (1983), *The Anglican Spiritual Tradition*, London, Darton, Longman and Todd.

Pollard, A and Hennell, M (eds) (1959), *Charles Simeon, 1759–1836*, London, SPCK.

Rowell, G (1983), *The Vision Glorious*, Oxford, Oxford University Press.

Turtle, R G (1978), *John Wesley: his life and theology*, Grand Rapids, Michigan, Zondervan.

Walker, A K (1973), *William Law: his life and thought*, London, SPCK.

6. MISSION IN AN INDIFFERENT WORLD

Introduction

The development of an Anglican tradition in terms of Church structures and personal spirituality was realistic, in recognising that many of those who were invited and included nonetheless seemed content to remain at a distance and ignore the possibilities of the Gospel. This situation became particularly acute in the eighteenth century, when the Anglican Church seemed moribund and the revival movements tended to be critical of its inclusive structures and spirituality. Joseph Butler produced an important apologetic for the Anglican tradition which continues to provide resources often ignored by the narrow party approaches to mission within Anglicanism.

Reflecting on experience

Think of the life and processes of any part of Nature, such as a daffodil bulb.
• What can they tell us about creation?
• What is missing from these reflections in terms of a *Christian* understanding of creation?
• Is there an essential continuity or discontinuity between the 'natural' and the 'supernatural'?

EXERCISE

📖 **Read Acts 5:1–16.** What might this passage tell us about the responsibilities of believers and their relationship with others? You might consider the following points:
   • the contrast between natural instincts ('touched by Satan', 'fallen') and the higher aims of the Gospel (which are inspired by Christ as Messiah); ▶▶

- the connection between sin, judgement and death;
- the role of the apostles in clarifying discernment;
- the distinction between the believers and others who did not dare to join them, but spoke highly of them;
- the attractiveness of the Messiah and his Gospel as focused in the believers;
- the healing of infirmities in Nature by the grace of God, mediated by the apostle;
- the relationship between the group of believers and those who come for healing.

Joseph Butler (1692–1752)

Joseph Butler was born into a presbyterian family and thus he pursued his education initially in what was then called 'a dissenting academy' in Gloucester. One of his fellow students was Thomas Secker, later Archbishop of Canterbury. In 1714 Butler became an Anglican and went to Oriel College in Oxford. By 1718 he was ordained and appointed as preacher at the Rolls Chapel in London. In 1726 he published *Fifteen Sermons Preached at the Rolls Chapel*, which became a standard text for moral philosophy.

After seven years as incumbent of Stanhope in the Diocese of Durham, during which time he published *The Analogy of Religion*, he was appointed Bishop of Bristol in 1738. The endowment of that see was inadequate for the proper discharge of episcopal responsibilities but this was remedied in 1740 when he was also made Dean of St Paul's in London. (It was quite common in the eighteenth century for clerics to hold a number of posts in order to make an adequate living.) He became Bishop of Durham in 1750. Two incidents in Butler's life may serve to illustrate his theology.

The ordinary is adequate

When he was the Bishop of Durham, a local gentleman sought his advice. Butler was very busy but said that the man could come and have lunch with him. Not surprisingly the man put on his best clothes and went to Auckland Castle expecting a very fine occasion. Later, in his diary, the man wrote of his great disappointment because the lunch was simply the two of them, on a very small table, and he recorded 'it was just meat and pudding'. Butler told him that he always ate simply because that was enough for anyone. Meat and pudding was enough: the ordinary and the basic is adequate.

Investing in the truth

The second story also comes from his time in Durham. A man who was setting up a charitable scheme to help needy people came to visit him as Bishop. He listened very carefully as the man explained what the scheme would achieve, what it required and how it would help the needy. He was impressed and calling his steward he asked, 'How much money have I got?' The steward replied: 'You have £500 sir.' Joseph Butler responded: '£500, what a shame for a bishop to have so much money. Give it all to this man for his charitable plan' (Bartlett, 1839, p. 197).

Joseph Butler was always concerned for beggars and those in need and when he recognised a scheme worth investing in he put his trust and his money into it, as a way of satisfying human need and fulfilling the Gospel. Here are important emphases on working with others, generosity and investing in appropriate schemes wholeheartedly.

EXERCISE

What do you find significant in these two stories about Bishop Butler in terms of his exemplifying something important in being Anglican?

The emergence of the modern world

The eighteenth century is often characterised as an 'age of reason'. There are important parallels with our own time, especially if we substitute the term 'scientific culture' for 'reason'. In both periods the great emphasis is upon human experience: the ability to measure, order and effect. As confidence in these capabilities grows, 'faith' seems irrelevant and Scripture and Christian doctrine are often found wanting at the bar of reason.

In the preface to his seminal work *The Analogy of Religion*, Joseph Butler wrote that people set up Christianity 'as a principal subject of mirth and ridicule, as it were by way of reprisals, for its having so long interrupted the pleasures of the world' (Butler, 1897, p. 2). We may note a number of reasons for this hostility to Christianity, many of which are reflected in the modern world.

In the seventeenth century people fought for their faith. Religious wars were deeply destructive, including the Civil War in England. As a result, religious belief became marginalised from public life in the name of toleration. Religion was to be a private and domestic experience. Public life was to be ordered by reason and good sense: *common* human qualities. Christianity soon produced an appropriate theology, which came to be known as 'Deism'. God was seen as a First Cause, a clock-maker responsible for the wonderful intricacy of creation, which humanity was now responsible for ordering and overseeing.

The philosopher Thomas Hobbes (1588–1679) argued that the state of humankind is basically that of selfishness: we are naturally in a state of competition and war with one another. The only way to counteract this tendency is to enter into a social contract. Covenanting with others to try to create peace will establish a Sovereign Power. In other words, people make their own God to rule the public domain. In *The Fable of the Bees* (1723), Bernard de Mandeville argued that private vices are public virtues. The world obtains its energy and creativity through self-ishness and competition.

EXERCISE

To what extent are these factors of selfishness, rationalism and competition incompatible with Christianity?

Butler's response: not rational but personal

In his *Fifteen Sermons* Joseph Butler argued that humankind is not nat-urally selfish, competitive and driven by cool reason. Essentially we are made with more personal qualities, which go beyond the confines of reason and self-interest. He contends that there is a deep and common instinct in human beings rooted in our feelings of love, compassion and justice, which needs to go alongside our capacities for reason and self-ishness.

This can be illustrated by the example of someone walking by a river when a child falls into the water. The great majority of human beings instinctively will leap in to save the child. We will not stop and reason, asking, 'What is the risk to me?', 'Can I swim strongly enough?', 'How fast is the current?', 'How heavy is the child?' Rather, we have an instinct sim-ply to leap in and try to rescue the child. This is an instinct to reach out to need that is more fundamental to human beings than the essentially selfish and corrupt 'nature' identified by commentators such as Hobbes and de Mandeville (Bernard, 1900, Vol. II, p. 3). For Joseph Butler, beneath these kinds of sentiment there is something deeper and richer (which is of God) that we must recognise and cultivate, binding us to others and to the purposes of creation rather than setting us against one another. It is in the very nature and constitution of things to bind us to others in a profound oneness, shown most clearly in our instinctive reaction to the reality of human need (Cunliffe, 1992, p. 150).

He goes on to argue that this is a sign of a God who is not just a first cause underwriting a rational universe. Rather this instinct for oneness points to a God who has given us these qualities of feeling towards others, this ability to reach out to others. These instincts in us reflect the realities of the God who makes and sustains us. Therefore God is certainly a person, not a first cause: a person endowed with all the most perfect moral qualities which we can merely begin to grasp through our deepest instincts and experiences.

EXERCISE

Do you feel that humanity is basically motivated by selfishness or by a desire to give of self for the sake of others? How can these sentiments be assessed and weighed?

Do you prefer to describe God in terms that are:
- personal ('father', 'comforter' etc.); or
- impersonal ('almighty', 'omnipotent' etc.)?

Are the differences between these two ways of describing God important for mission?

The 'Analogy of Religion'

Joseph Butler wishes to take seriously our human ability to reason and to reflect on experience, which are the tools of modern life. As a Christian minister, he is equally committed to take seriously the revelation of the Christian faith: grace from outside ourselves and the mystery of atonement. He was keen to avoid the trap of much modern theology, which upholds a Christianity of incarnation for which God is present in human experience, but is uncomfortable with notions of judgement and grace from beyond this world. In the *Analogy of Religion* he brings together these two concerns in a creative and challenging way, both for secular rationalists and for Christian believers.

Reason and revelation

Joseph Butler begins by stating that both reason and revelation depend upon what he calls 'probability'. This is especially interesting in our own times because much of modern science has come increasingly to recognise that its own findings are based on 'probability' rather than on what we might call absolute certainty. Further, scientific theories change and develop as new evidence or perspectives are discovered. For him, both the human ability to understand and reason about what is given to us in Nature, and our ability to receive revelation, are based on probability. This is important because among his contemporaries some held that reason was absolute, while traditional Church people held that revelation was absolute. Butler argues that both work on probability, which means that we are always in the position of being *potential learners*. There is always more to learn from reason and from revelation: neither provides absolute answers. The probability factor means that there is always more to be discerned and discovered, and each person is always a potential learner. This continues the insights of Hooker and Laud with regard to development and change.

A necessary wholeness

Joseph Butler is keen to establish that revelation not only involves the same kind of knowing as reason, but also that we need Nature to help us understand revelation and we need revelation to help us understand Nature. Each needs the other.

The problems and possibilities we have in discovering the purpose and properties of Nature will mirror the problems and possibilities we have in discovering the purposes and properties of revelation. In this way Nature and revelation inform each other and need to be held together. This poses a challenge to a rationalistic world keen to ignore religion and to a defensive Church tempted to overrule and ignore reason to protect 'faith' as a gift of revelation.

Joseph Butler is unequivocal that in seeking to discover the truth about God and the Gospel we cannot pick and choose. There is a wholeness about this process that has to be recognised and accepted, since human experience is not just about the 'now' but must be truly seen within the wider context of creation and what has been given.

In the *Analogy of Religion*, therefore, he explores the question of whether or not the experience of being human confirms or refutes what religious revelation teaches.

EXERCISE
How would you assess the distinction between 'reason' and 'revelation'?

The Christian revelation

In outlining the 'wholeness' of revelation according to the Christian religion, Joseph Butler focuses upon six key elements, which can be tested against human experience.

1. Humankind is appointed to live towards a future state.
2. Everyone is to be rewarded or punished according to their behaviour in this life.
3. Thus this present life is a time of probation, a state of trial and a discipline for a future life.
4. Humanity objects to there being any kind of moral plan or government because it does not seem to be very clearly made known to us. There is something that seems to stop us from clearly understanding that we are called to live in a future state, that this present life is a time of trial and that we will be rewarded or punished for our behaviour. Hence revelation teaches that the human condition is corrupt.
5. Because there is something that is corrupt about us, preventing clear recognition of these factors, there needs to be some extra dispensation from our creator. This extra help is provided by miracles and by a Messiah.
6. These miracles and this Messiah do not reveal the fullness of truth to all people, but only to a part of humankind.

Does revelation match human experience?

Having outlined these key features of the Christian revelation, Joseph Butler proceeds to explore the natural world to see if it relates to this process and purpose. His method is based upon probability and upon an insistence that the exploration must examine the whole process, not just parts of it.

Appointed to live towards a future state. First, he tests the element of revelation that indicates that we are made for a future state, beyond this world. If we examine the experience of humanity there are some indications that such a process could be probable. He points to worms becoming flies, birds bursting from their shells into a new and totally different world, and our own experience of dramatic change and development, not just from the womb, but from infancy to maturity.

He concedes that this evidence from human experience is not conclusive regarding the issue of a future state; but because this matter is so important for us, reason and prudence would advise that we pursue the matter further, not least because Nature provides signs pointing to such a probability. In terms of the two stories at the beginning of this chapter, it is important to take seriously both that the ordinary is adequate ('meat and pudding') and also that the search for someone with a trustworthy scheme for salvation is essential.

Reward or punishment. Second, if we accept that there might be a future life, the question arises as to how it might be related to this present existence. Joseph Butler shows that there is a strong tendency in human beings to reward good behaviour and to punish evil in this life, and also to have a sense that such issues may be part of a greater reckoning. He uses the illustration of the way in which Nature gives us faculties which produce pain when we do things to damage our bodies (for example putting our fingers in fire). If our creator has thus made our natural bodies, it is probable that our moral selves are made in the same way, that is to learn through reward or punishment. This is how we treat children.

This evidence from human experience and reason shows that there is nothing incredible in a revelation of a God who will punish and reward people for their actions. Even contemporaries like Hobbes recognised that it is prudent for human well-being to reward good behaviour and to punish evil. This is the message of Christian revelation too.

Thus the first two elements of the Christian revelation accord closely with the experience of being human and observing the natural world:
• the evidence for a future state, development and change;
• the evidence for a sense of reward and punishment.

Joseph Butler has appealed to human experience, prudence, self-interest and the importance of probability.

EXERCISE
Is it true in your experience that human beings have a real interest
in the possibility of a future life?

Do notions of reward and punishment feature more prominently
in the world rather than in the life and witness of the Church?
What might this imply?

A time of trial. According to Butler's argument, the third element of
revelation is that this present life is a time of *probation*: a testing as part
of being perfected to a higher state. Once again he asserts that human
experience bears testimony to this instinct and aspiration – a desire for
greater perfection motivates the forces of government and culture and
is worked out by testing and trial, wrestling with vice and virtue (needing punishment and reward) and looking to an improved future state.
He argues that we start in life unfinished, needing *acquired* qualifications of knowledge and experience to fit us for another life. 'The constitution of human creatures . . . is such, as that they are capable of
naturally becoming qualified for states of life, for which they were once
wholly unqualified' (Butler, 1897, p. 90).

The corruption of the human condition. Fourth, it is at this point that
Joseph Butler recognises that human experience might begin to diverge
from the story of revelation. We may have intimations of a future life, of
reward and punishment and of this life as a time of trial, but there is no
real clarity. As we struggle in Nature with these things, he says, we must
expect to struggle with revelation. But according to the canons of
human experience, prudence and self-interest, reason teaches us that if
revelation seems to be so close to our own observations then it is important to explore what further revelation offers, because of the significance
of the issues at stake.

EXERCISE
How far is it true in your own experience that each of us has
'intimations of this life as a time of trial'? Can you give examples?

The Messiah and miracles. Fifth, we move in our testing of the story of revelation to the extra dimensions that it adds to what is known through basic human experience. In terms of Christianity, our intimations about a future life, reward and punishment, and this life as a time of trial, are evidence of God the Father Almighty, the creator. But what distinguishes Christianity, and thus offers something unique to humankind, is the Gospel of the Messiah and the power of miracles: in terms of Christian theology, the Son and the Holy Spirit.

> The essence of natural religion may be said to consist in religious regards to God the Father Almighty: and the essence of revealed religion, as distinguished from natural, to consist in religious regards to the Son, and to the Holy Ghost . . . The Son and the Spirit have each his proper office in the great dispensation of Providence, the redemption of the world; the one our Mediator, the other our Sanctifier. (Butler, 1897, p. 164)

Joseph Butler shows that the questions raised by reason and human experience find an answer in this revelation, which gives clarity and sense unattainable simply on our own. Christ 'published anew the law of nature . . . He taught mankind, taught us authoritatively, to live soberly, righteously and godly in this present world, in expectation of the future judgement of God. He confirmed the truth of this moral system of nature' (Butler, 1897, pp. 219–220). But Christ goes further because he invites us to a Kingdom which is beyond this world, he founded a Church to offer invitation to it and he made himself a sacrifice for human failings, atonement for the sins of the world.

He accepts that there is much debate about how to explain this fact, but adds:

> I do not find that the scripture has explained it . . . Some have endeavoured to explain the efficacy of what Christ has done and suffered for us, beyond what the scripture has authorised: others, probably because they could not explain it, have been for taking it away, and confining his office as Redeemer of the world to his instruction, example, and governance of the church. Whereas the doctrine of the gospel appears to be, not only that he taught the efficacy of repentance, but rendered it of the efficacy which it is, by what he did and suffered for us: that he obtained for us the benefit of having our repentance accepted unto eternal life: not only that he revealed to sinners that they were in a capacity of salvation, and how they might obtain it; but

moreover that he put them into this capacity of salvation, by what he did and suffered for them; put us into a capacity of escaping future punishment, and obtaining future happiness. And it is our wisdom thankfully to accept the benefit, by performing the conditions upon which it is offered on our part, without disputing how it was procured on his. (Butler, 1897, pp. 221–222)

These words repay careful study. They summarise Joseph Butler's case that the Christ not only models and fulfils the instinct and impetus known in human experience and in Nature, towards a future state, through probation or trial and the conflicting claims of virtue and vice. Christ in his Person and his Spirit also empowers us to accept this way and to know in him its victory and completion, through the sign of his resurrection from suffering and death and the power of his Holy Spirit to so transform and enlighten human kind.

EXERCISE
How do you react to Joseph Butler's argument about the Messiah bringing proper completion to the forces of creation?

A holy remnant. Sixth and last, Joseph Butler recognises that God has raised up a corporation, the followers of this Messiah. Their task is to hold on to this truth in the story of the Messiah and the ongoing miracle of resurrection which has been intimated in so many ways, to present this story to others to be a framework for making sense of their experience of being human, and to call people to trust their instincts that this way can fulfil their desire for a more righteous and fulfilled existence.

Thus the Church (the few) has a very important role in recalling and representing the story and miracle of the Messiah, and the manifestations of his Spirit enhancing and fulfilling nature. The Messiah, the miracles (expressions of the Spirit calling Nature to resurrection) and the Church show us the deeper relations and potential within which we stand. In prudence, self-interest and according to the canons of probability, we should take these extra dispensations with the utmost seriousness.

The call to serious investment

This process is illustrated by the story of the man who came to see Bishop Butler to explain his scheme for helping people in need – a human example of mediation as a real part of our nature and experience. The man outlined the scheme, but the Bishop did not go to see it working for he had an intuition that it could fulfil its claims from what he already knew of human nature and from resonating with the way in which the man presented it. Two things connect and complete each other: the bishop's own experience of human living and the vision and call of the man with this scheme for the future. Joseph Butler says in effect, therefore, 'Yes, this need is so great and I am convinced that the scheme seems designed to meet this need and is worth trying. Thus I will invest everything in it – here is my £500.'

And this is Joseph Butler's call to others in relation to the Christian message. The Church comes like the man in the story, saying that there is a certain human need and experience, and that there is a scheme of revelation which can take these things seriously and lead to fulfilment and wholeness, beyond the terms of this world and our narrow human experience. For this to happen it is essential to invest everything in the scheme that is offered. The response has to be, 'How much have I got? Put it all in this scheme.' Whatever we possess, we must give it all to this way of living and believing, and by doing so we receive the grace of eternity. The story can be a parable of how Butler sees the Church helping the individual to make a decision and to follow it through. This individual decision is based on the experience of being human, the aspiration for a future life, consciousness of the struggle between good and evil and of being in a state of trial, and connecting this with the revelation in a Father, a Messiah and the miracle of the Spirit. The Church has a role to proclaim the story of revelation and encourage others to accept it and invest all they have in it. As with Hooker and Laud, this process is dynamic, not static.

Mission in the modern world

Joseph Butler's case is as important for the twenty-first century as for the eighteenth. The Church is not trying to offer people something that is totally foreign to them, nor is it asking people to change and forget who they are and where they have come from in order to become totally different, which is sometimes the way in which we present the faith through evangelism. Rather, Butler holds that the Church stands for a scheme of revelation that connects with the deepest experience and aspiration of being human. In this sense incarnation and atonement meet.

The deepest questions that every human being asks are these:
- 'Is there more? Is there a future?'
- 'What is this within me which struggles with good and evil?'
- 'Is my life some kind of trial or probation?'

Many religions and philosophers have recognised these fundamental questions. For Butler the Christian revelation begins with these issues about the human condition, but then takes us from such real and everyday experience towards those things of which we have an intuition and a hope when we stop to reflect more deeply. The Gospel confirms that these issues are fundamental and encourages us to recognise that they do not simply relate to creation (in religious language, to God the Father). There is, further, a Messiah and there is a miracle, there is the Son and the Holy Spirit, who give a fuller answer to our questions – and that is the good news. Each individual needs to come to this recognition and decision, but all can be carried along by the corporation which is the Church.

Joseph Butler's work is profoundly scriptural and rooted in the revelation of the Messiah who cleanses and gives comfort. He holds that the Christian religion connects with prudence, self-interest and the probability inherent in human experience, but it is a whole package and we cannot choose the parts which attract us, such as Christmas and Harvest which affirm creation, without reflecting on the Messiah and miracle as focused in Good Friday and Easter.

Here is a message that both affirms and challenges the inclusive parochial spirituality of Anglicanism.

EXERCISE

What do you think of the six elements in Joseph Butler's understanding of Christian revelation?

Can his understanding of the complementarity of (a) the basic questions in human being (Is there more? Is there a future? What is this within me which struggles with good and evil? Is my life some kind of a trial?) and (b) the Gospel of Messiah and miracle, be the basis of mission for today?

How does his notion of the Church relate to your own understanding of the nature and task of a parish?

The task of the Church

The commission to those called to be the Church is to help others recognise that the story of the Messiah, his life, death and resurrection, and the miracle of the Holy Spirit, are the factors which connect most truly with the basic questions that human experience confronts.

For Joseph Butler this task is to be fulfilled by means of the word preached, the sacraments administered, a settled public liturgy, a church building, the use of special occasions for teaching and parental responsibility for the Christian nurture of children.

Joseph Butler is in the tradition of Hooker, Herbert and Laud in stressing that the Gospel is not about signs of what some may become, rather it is about participation in a process on which all human beings are embarked. All are potential learners. He challenged the Christianity of his day with being obsessed by its own institutional life and an overemphasis upon God as creator. He felt that these concerns failed to engage with the real questions by which people live, and thus did not give proper witness to the Messiah and to miracle. These are the keys to the Church's mission in the modern world.

EXERCISE

Joseph Butler saw an essential dynamic between:
- acknowledging our finiteness (as creatures of a creator); and
- acknowledging our aspiration for the infinite (the good news of the Messiah and the miracle of the Holy Spirit).

Can this be a useful framework for understanding the task of an inclusive Church in the modern world?

📖 **Read Acts 5:17–42.** In terms of Joseph Butler's missionary strategy and understanding of the role of the Church, what thoughts does this passage prompt? You may like to note the following points:
- In the conflict between the party of the High Priest and the apostles, the latter are 'saved' by an angel of the Lord – something beyond the bounds of apparently normal human experience.
- This 'Gospel' of salvation is to be proclaimed in the temple: the heart of established beliefs.   ▶▶

- The point at issue is teaching in the name of Jesus Christ, the Messiah.
- This Messiah is crucial to human salvation, as focused in the process of death and resurrection.
- This process becomes the model for Christian living: the apostles were imprisoned and then freed by God, flogged and then raised anew.
- This is the miracle of salvation – the outpouring of the power of the Holy Spirit in the midst of human experience of conflict, struggle and need.

Further reading

Bartlett, T (1839), *Memoirs of Joseph Butler*, London, J W Parker.

Bernard, J H (1900), *The Works of Bishop Butler*, London, Macmillan.

Butler, J (1897), *The Analogy of Religion*, ed. W E Gladstone, Oxford, Clarendon.

Cunliffe, C (ed.) (1992), *Joseph Butler's Moral and Religious Thought*, Oxford, Clarendon.

Holland, H S (1908), *The Optimism of Butler's 'Analogy'*, Oxford, Clarendon.

Penelhum, T (1985), *Butler*, London, Routledge and Kegan Paul.

Ramsey, I (1969), *Joseph Butler 1692-1752*, London, Dr William's Trust.

Rurak, J (1980), Butler's Analogy: a still interesting synthesis of reason and revelation, *Anglican Theological Review*, LXII, 4, 365–381.

7. RE-FORMING ANGLICAN IDENTITY

Introduction

The nineteenth century brought to a head the paradox of vigorous Christian revival in a world increasingly confident in its own scientific secularism. There was an urgent need for the Anglican Church to re-assess its establishment role and to discern how best to order and promote itself as an agent of an inclusive Gospel in an increasingly divided and indifferent environment. The steady growth of liberalism in politics and morality provided a culture of easy accommodation. Boundaries and identity needed to be asserted, not simply through revivalist calls towards a renewed emphasis upon pulpit or sacraments, but through a realistic engagement with the very worldliness of industrial society. The person who articulated this Anglican emphasis most clearly was Charles Gore.

Reflecting on experience

What makes membership of the army distinctive? Why is this distinctiveness important? Why is it dangerous?

EXERCISE

📖 **Read Acts 6:1–7.** What might this story tell us about boundaries, distinctiveness and ministerial strategy? Consider especially:
- the need for different roles and functions, which will be complementary;
- change stemming from recognising human need and those not normally noticed;
- decision-making by the whole group of believers together;
- priority given to preaching God's word and to prayer;
- candidates for this ministry being presented by the group and authorised by the apostles.

Charles Gore (1853–1932)

Gore was educated at Oxford where he became a tutor, lecturing on Plato. He moved to be Vice-Principal of the Theological College of Cuddesdon and then became the first Principal of Pusey House in Oxford. However, he was no cloistered academic; he had a deep concern for the sufferings and struggles of industrial society, where religion was a private matter and secular forces were gaining momentum. He was successively a parish priest, a canon of Westminster and Bishop of Worcester, Birmingham and Oxford. He thus worked at the heart of the establishment. However, he consistently strove to challenge the complacency of the Church of England and to draw more creatively on the resources of the Anglican tradition in this new environment.

His interests and his influence can be grasped from three initiatives in which he played a key role.

The Christian Social Union

Gore founded this movement with Westcott and Scott Holland in 1889. The objectives of the Union were:

- to claim for the Christian law the ultimate authority to rule social practice;
- to study in common how to apply the moral truths and principles of Christianity to the social and economic difficulties of the present time;
- to present Christ in practical life as the living master and king, the enemy of wrong and selfishness, the power of righteousness and love (Reardon, 1971, p. 470).

We should note the emphasis he laid upon law and authority, society as well as individuals, research and development, and the Messiah.

The Community of the Resurrection

Initially established by Gore in rural Oxfordshire in 1892, the community soon moved to Mirfield near Leeds. Gore worked to provide an appropriate framework for Christian ministry there, based upon a distinctive discipline of common prayer, simple lifestyle, engagement with social need and opportunities for study and learning. He saw that these distinctive marks of Christian living need to be modelled as witness and invitation to a world that was increasingly estranged from the Church and her task.

A religion of incarnation

In 1889 Gore edited a book of essays entitled *Lux Mundi: a series of studies in the religion of incarnation*. This illustrates his desire to work with and learn from others (for ministry is a collaborative enterprise), to make the doctrine of God being born in human flesh the basis of mission and ministry, and to recognise the ongoing need for study and exploration so as to better connect the Gospel with the world.

Gore was clear that the Church should begin with the incarnation, but he was fierce in his insistence that the challenge of judgement, the call to repentance and the offer of atonement were equally vital. He understood the Anglican tradition as being a form of 'scriptural catholicism', witnessing to the spirit of prophecy which calls individuals and organisations to exercise that moral judgement which is foundational to human being. For Gore, the key prophetic task of the Church and her ministry is to help focus the connection between the word of God which is given 'from outside' and the consciences of those who by receiving this revelation give it enfleshment and authentication in this world. He saw Jesus as the culmination of the prophetic tradition.

EXERCISE

How would you evaluate the aims of the Christian Social Union? Are they realistic?

How do you understand Jesus and the prophetic tradition in Scripture?

The prophetic distinctiveness of the Church

Gore accepted the teaching of Hooker and Laud about the inclusiveness of God's scheme for salvation. He agreed that each element within this scheme needs to discern and fulfil the key part it plays both in itself and for the well-being of the whole. However, in an age when the myth of Christendom was being exposed, he drew on the tradition of Herbert, Law and Butler to explore the importance of Christian distinctiveness for the sake of the whole, and the potential for each person to connect with the all-embracing word of God, since God's call to a greater fulfilment in the Messiah exactly matched the deepest human aspirations.

For Gore this prophetic distinctiveness, crucial to the well-being of both Church and world, was focused in three key areas: maintaining appropriate boundaries, being open to new things and practising proper unity and order.

Boundaries

Just as leaven and salt are only effective through being distinctive, so Gore recognised that Christians could only play their particular roles in the scheme of salvation if they were properly conscious of what such a vocation should involve.

He uses the distinction between minorities and majorities. Gore argues that God works through minorities. That is the theme of the Old Testament: tiny Israel is chosen to have a vocation linked to the salvation of the nations. Israel constantly succumbs to the temptation to limit her concerns to her own life, but the prophets remind her that she has been given blessings for the sake of the whole.

Similarly Jesus preached to everyone, but in parables. This was an inclusive method, but only a few understood and gathered round him to be trained as a small group to be leaven in the world. Jesus works through a minority: a small group that exists to model and to proclaim something for the rest of humankind. This small group can only fulfil such a function if it is distinctive. Like a city set on a hill, it has to be marked by separation from what Gore calls 'the surrounding masses': both for the sake of itself, having integrity in its own witness as a remnant, and also for the sake of those who need this deeper perspective and confidence to enlighten their own most basic intuitions. Jesus had 'a profound contempt for majorities' (this was written in a time of great concern for universal suffrage!) (Gore, 1930, p. 192) and developed this method of the minority, that is those who were prepared to give their all for the Kingdom. Jesus created a spiritual aristocracy, and mission for Gore became the claim that 'what we want is not more Christians but better Christians' (Gore, 1898, p. 190).

Gore recognised in his own day that the Church must be distinctive in regard to the life of society and thus in relation to the State, since establishment blurred the boundaries between the Gospel, which the Church stands for, and the world in which it is set.

EXERCISE

What do you think about Gore's insistence that God works through minorities? How does this notion relate to the role of an established Church?

The boundary markers

To maintain these boundaries the Church must have a distinctive creed, distinctive worship, a distinctive moral law and a distinctive social life. Together these provide the basis of Christian mission. Gore recognised the tendency, that was later to become increasingly prevalent, of the Church trying to blur the boundaries in these four areas. He knew that in the Anglican tradition boundaries should be permeable, but warned that if access was too easy much would be lost. Gore reminds us that in the early Church, which was set in a hostile world, converts spent a long period in instruction and training before being allowed to attend the Eucharist. This vividly contrasts with the current desire for instant access and communion for children!

Gore was especially emphatic about the importance of a distinctive moral law and social life.

> There exists what can rightly be called a Christian socialism, by the very fact that the law of brotherhood is the law of Christ. It is quite beyond all question that according to the intention of Christ, the Christian Church should at all times represent a body living not only by a certain rule of faith, but also by a certain moral law, which puts the sternest restraints upon the spirit of competition, on the acquisition of wealth, on selfish aggrandisement: which bids every man, in the simplest sense, love his neighbour as himself, which enjoins the bearing of one another's burdens, as the only fulfilling of the law of Christ . . . The prophetic function of the church as it seems to me, at the present moment, is not so much, in the first instance, to expand Christian influence as to concentrate it. (Gore, 1891, p. 211)

Gore called himself 'a Christian Socialist', meaning that Christians should stand for a radical co-operation and fellowship that is distinctive from the competitive, individualistic way in which the world normally works. The first Christians were distinctive for the quality of their fellowship and the purity of their sexual ethics. God works through us and in us as love, not as authority or orthodoxy. Thus, for Gore, the key issue was moral witness. This is why he eventually resigned as Bishop of Oxford over the question of whether those who could take an active role in forming the Church should be the baptised or only the confirmed. He believed that the confirmed should take seriously the practice of faith, in an adult and distinctive way.

Gore worried about cheap, nominal communion between the Church and the greater number of people in society. It helped neither the Church, nor those who were so loosely connected with it, since there was no real leaven in the relationship. All had been diluted. The task of our times was to resist this tendency, he argued. In the name of Christ, the Church must make the obligations of membership real:

> To be a member of the church must be understood to involve not only financial obligations, though it involves that, but also all that is implied in active membership of a society which is entrusted with an exacting message to a reluctant world . . . it is in proportion as the obligation of membership is accepted, that the right of the whole laity to share in the government of the church can be recognised and can have real expression given to it. In fact the loss of the true position and dignity of the laity has been due in history not so much to clerical aggression, as to the lowering of the standard of lay membership. (Gore, 1909, p. 72)

Gore recognises that 'the church has never been in the habit of scrutinising the orthodoxy of its lay members. It is certainly undesirable that it should do so today. But there is no similar objection to emphasising their practical obligations' (Gore, 1909, p. 73).

Thus he acknowledges the freedom of lay people to explore the meaning and expression of faith. But it is clear that a distinctive social and moral life are not so negotiable, since Christianity is a faith of incarnation, of God's life becoming flesh in us, and of atonement, of our being forgiven and made one with God and filled with new life, so that we become agents of that life in the world in which we are set. To be a Christian has radical practical consequences because of the part each person plays within the holy fellowship of the Church and in relation to the world outside.

EXERCISE
Do you agree with Gore that distinctive moral and social standards are more important to lay Christians than conformity to doctrinal orthodoxy?

The boundary between Church and world is located and maintained in these four areas of distinctiveness, which keep the Church as a minority modelling a way of life and inviting others to share it. Hence the work of the Christian Social Union and the Community of the Resurrection: both very significant titles, as well as very influential enterprises, that stem from Gore.

The call to reform for the Kingdom in the face of so much that defiled and stunted the image of God in so many of his creatures would proceed, Gore wrote, 'not by methods of majorities, but from small groups of sanctified men' (Gore, 1892, p. 8). Despite the inevitable sexism of his language, Gore prophetically challenged the uncritical faith in democracy which marked his time and which still stands as a persuasive idol today.

Yet Gore was realistic in a manner that should offer consolation to Anglicans overwhelmed by the statistics of decline. He acknowledges that this approach would not bring the world flooding into the Church. Jesus had 'a profound contempt for majorities'; God had always worked through minorities. There was little evidence from Scripture or Church history that those who actually held the Gospel with integrity would ever be more than a small number. The world needed leaven, according to Gore. The leaven must be distinctive and make its contribution. This allowed enormous freedom under God's grace for how it seemed to be used or abused. We can see the inclusive, world-affirming theology of F D Maurice influencing Gore here. Yet the minority needs a sharp edge, a real distinctiveness over against the majority.

The implications for the Christian way

Gore was clear that to fulfil this essentially missionary role, and to strive after the integrity to which God calls the minority, the Church of England had to address a number of key tasks:

- to clarify and strengthen the obligations of membership;
- to make explicit the task and duty of the clergy;
- to ensure that the Church exercises government herself and is not subject to the State (the majority);
- to recover an emphasis upon prophecy. Gore recognised that the inevitable tendency of ministry and of institutional life is to emphasise quiescence and caring, and avoid disturbance;
- to recover Christian communion, the importance of the ecumenical enterprise;
- to assert the priority of practice as focused in the challenge of the needy. 'Practice' of this nature was the mark of Christian distinctiveness. Gore showed how Jesus in his parables allowed intellectual openness and exploration, but pointed to illustrations of challenging, disturbing practice;

- to take revelation seriously in ordinary and struggling human beings, often so as to expand and develop the Church's own insights. Gore wrote, 'Jesus exhibited the profoundest confidence in the capacity of the ordinary labouring man, without special education, if only the will be good, to apprehend the highest truth about God and humanity, right and wrong, sin and salvation' (Gore, 1909, p. 21);
- to recognise that truth is aristocratic, not democratic. Anglican inclusiveness in outreach is always balanced by the facts about Jesus. Gore observed, 'no teacher of the common people ever more conspicuously preferred spiritual truth to popularity and success. After a time he even adopted a method of teaching by parables which sifted out the genuine spirits who would search for and ponder the inner meaning, from the careless mass. Only he that had ears to hear should hear' (Gore, 1909, p. 22).

This reformed identity was crucial to the Anglican Church being true to its vocation as a national Church exercising an active responsibility towards every citizen. How others reacted to this witness of challenge and invitation was in God's hands and not to be measured by human standards. It was acceptable to be a minority with a universal concern. Here we see Hooker and Laud's theology given a scriptural, properly catholic and post-Christendom identity.

EXERCISE
Comment on the implications of Gore's views for the Christian life.

Is Christianity compatible with democracy?

Boundaries within the Church

Just as Christians are called to distinctiveness in the world, so within the corporation of the Church there is a God-given variety of gifts and commissions. Crucial to Gore was the distinction between clergy and laity. Clergy were called, trained and appointed to stand for the teaching which 'moulds' the individual experience of grace and provides a benchmark for the authenticity of Christian experience, giving shape and focus for dialogue as people travel on their various journeys to discover and fulfil their potential in the most appropriate way. Thus clergy should stand with integrity for the doctrines and formulas judged by the Church at that time as essential to measure and connect the experience of grace with the authentic story of Jesus living, dying and rising.

By contrast, individual lay Christians need space to develop and explore faith in the Christian journey, and in relation to their secular contexts, but always rooted in the common life and worship of the Church. Such a variety of wrestling, exploring and experimenting was inevitable: 'It has never been the habit of the church to scrutinise the orthodoxy of its lay members' (Gore, 1909, p. 73).

Here we see Gore developing Herbert's idea of a distinctive Christian community which worshipped and worked on behalf of the wider parish, as well as Law's notion of 'little societies'. Gore recognised that the well-being of such salt-like enterprises required a common focus of belief and worship safeguarded by an authorised leadership, so as to allow enormous freedom in the exploring of individual vocations and the making of an appropriate witness in such a variety of contexts.

EXERCISE
Do you think that Gore's distinction between clergy and laity is helpful in the modern Church?

Openness to new thinking

True to Anglican tradition, Gore's understanding of the Church, her ministry and mission, was dynamic not static. Beliefs should be explored and developed, as should modes of practical witness. But Laud's point about public order and a deeper unity was also important. Gore argued that Anglicanism followed the tradition of the early Church in its approach to development and change. This method was what he called 'comparing independent testimonies'. He quoted Hooker: 'The divine mystery was more true than plain. Divers, having framed the same to their own conceits, and fancies, are found in their exposition thereof more plain than true' (Gore, 1905, p. 2).

We have an instinct to try to express the encounter with the mystery of God in ways that can give it focus and will allow the experience to be shared with others. This is important, but there is always a danger that our way of expressing something of the mystery of God (trying to make it 'plain') obscures the deeper reality which has so much more to teach us. Truth becomes circumscribed by our attempts to articulate it. We make an idol of our insights, rather than being open to further evidence of God's gift.

According to Gore, there are two ways of dealing with this inevitable tendency. Either we can accept a single, authoritative voice as interpreter, which is how he saw the Roman Catholic model with its increasing reliance upon the infallibility of the Pope (and thus of the priest). Or we can follow the example of the early Church councils, where Christians who had developed accounts of their experience of God's grace met to compare independent testimonies, to allow accretions to be removed and to agree a common approach under the guidance of the Holy Spirit.

Gore sees this method of comparing independent testimonies as distinctive of the Anglican tradition. It was at the root of the parish system, the oversight of the bishop of a diocese and the collegiality of bishops. At each level the wide range of experiences of grace, and the attempts to articulate them, were brought into creative dialogue around a commitment to common worship, the determinative influence of Scripture and the divinely appointed authority of the apostles to act as a focus and touchstone.

All of these factors were to be in a dynamic dialogue, but within the structures and order of a parochial and national Church. Laud's theology of 'further evidence' is given a framework within which development can proceed in a stable and unified way.

EXERCISE

How might the Church best operate a system for 'comparing independent testimonies'? What kind of adjudication would be necessary?

Unity

Gore highlights two key elements in understanding unity in such a Church. The first approach emphasises that the unity of the Church is not established by outward arrangements and structures, rather it depends upon what he calls 'the indwelling of the Spirit'. Following F D Maurice, he uses the example of a family, which is bonded not because of any arrangements to ensure physical proximity or regular encounters (as is the case in many of our presuppositions about modern liturgy!), but because of ties that transcend space and time. In a family there is 'a unity which underlies all external separations of place and time, a unity which underlies all external divisions and hostilities which result from the marring of the gift we are given by human sin' (Gore, 1905, p. 27).

Similarly, there is a deeper, spiritual unity amongst Christians and amongst all God's children. Like the branches rooted in one vine, it is the gift of Christ's life that makes all the different growths one. Here Gore follows Paul in asserting that the unity of the Church does not lie in subordination to one form of government: rather, it is rooted in the fact that the Church receives the one food – the life of Christ. This is how he interprets Paul's argument in 1 Corinthians 10. Thus Christians are made one by the indwelling of the Spirit, so that unity is essentially inward. We are called to express this unity outwardly. This unity has not yet been achieved; nonetheless, the deeper unity is a fact inwardly. Hence the importance of the discipline of common worship, whatever our differences.

Gore played a key role in re-establishing the teaching of Augustine about the way that the Eucharist embraces us in the body of Christ. Subsequent liturgical developments in Anglicanism have been based on this insight. Unity is received as a gift of grace in worship, not constructed or negotiated by our efforts.

The second approach is to recognise that there is a unity of truth. He quotes Romans 6:17: 'But thanks be to God that you who were once slaves of sin have become obedient from the heart to the form of teaching delivered to you.' For Gore, Christians are essentially formed by the form of teaching, 'sound words' or 'the mould' delivered to them. This teaching which 'moulds' or forms Christians 'in Christ' is committed to the Church through the apostles. Yet this common formation will produce believers who express their faith in different ways.

Thus apostles are important for two reasons. They are a symbol of unity, presiding over different Christian communities in the early Church and yet united in a common apostleship. Also, they are a symbol of the unity of truth, being guardians of the stories and teaching given to the Church and expressed essentially in Scripture.

EXERCISE

What are the problems of using the images of the vine and the body to describe Christian unity?

How does this issue relate to your reflections about the distinctiveness of the army?

How do you react to Gore's understanding of unity and identity?

📖 **Read Acts 7 and 8:1–17.** How does this account of a sharp distinction between Christians and others relate to Gore's thinking about re-forming Anglican identity? You may like to consider the following points.
- Stephen's speech confronts human stubbornness which wishes to ignore or resist God's prophetic actions and calling.
- Believers are dispersed, yet continue to witness to a single story.
- Philip witnesses to the Messiah and to miracles (the power of the Holy Spirit).
- The apostles have a particular role in giving focus to faith and confirming experiences of grace in the Holy Spirit. There is a wider collegiality and commonness in the faith, handled by the apostles.
- In the local context there is a clear distinction between the message and actions of believers, and the community in which they are set.

Further reading

Avis, P (1988), *Gore: construction and conflict*, Worthing, Churchman Publishing.

Carpenter, J (1960), *Gore: a study in liberal Catholic thought*, London, Faith Press.

Gore, C (1905), *Roman Catholic Claims*, London, Longmans, Green and Co.

Gore, C (1909), *Orders and Unity*, London, John Murray.

Gore, C (1930), *The Philosophy of the Good Life*, London, John Murray.

Hastings, A (1986), *A History of English Christianity 1920–1985*, London, Collins.

Ramsey, A M (1959), *From Gore to Temple*, London, Longman.

Reardon, B M G (1971), *Religious Thought in the Victorian Age*, London, Longman.

8. REVISING THE ROLE OF A NATIONAL CHURCH

Introduction

The call for Christian distinctiveness, from an established Church in an increasingly secular society, brought into play issues of prophecy and political involvement. The inclusiveness of a parochial spirituality needed to be balanced by a Gospel that confronted the need for change and repentance within a complex contemporary culture. This chapter is a case study of these issues, looking at the life of Josephine Butler and her concentration upon prayer as the bedrock of an appropriate Christian contribution to a society in which women were particularly abused and oppressed. She illustrates a new model for a national Church: evangelical energy from Church members expended for the sake of catholic principles and justice for all God's people, particularly the neglected and the marginalised.

Reflecting on experience
Think of something you have really desired and prayed for.
- How did you understand the role of prayer?
- How did you express your prayer/desire?
- How did this relate to other people?
- Is prayer only valid 'through Jesus Christ'?

EXERCISE
📖 **Read Acts 8:18–25.** What can we learn from this passage about prophecy, politics and prayer? You might like to consider:
- the difference between prayer and commercial transactions;
- repentance as the beginning of true prayer;

> - sin as a barrier to right thinking (prophecy), right acting (politics) and right desire (prayer);
> - that people can be helped by the prayers of others;
> - that the Gospel works through journeys, by people moving.

Josephine Butler (1828–1906)

Josephine Butler came from a radical family called the Greys. Her father was known for his support of the Reform Bill and the abolition of slavery. He was a firm believer in women's education and made a point of discussing social and political issues with his daughters. Josephine's mother was a strong evangelical and it is not surprising that her daughter grew up to display a deep mix of social concern and evangelical faith. Josephine and her sister Harriett were known as the 'belles of Northumberland' when they were in their teens, and they were criticised by the local gentry for riding too fast. That is a good image of Josephine Butler – an energetic woman who moved too fast for polite society.

When she was seventeen years old she went through some kind of 'dark night of the soul'. A few years later, as a young woman, she experienced a vision that was to be strangely prophetic for her adult life and for her understanding of prayer. She described it as follows:

> I heard a wailing cry somewhere among the trees in the twilight which was deepening into night. It was a woman's cry, a woman aspiring to heaven and dragged back to hell. And my heart was pierced with pain. I longed to leap from the window and flee with her to some place of refuge. I cannot explain the nature of the impression which remains with me to this day but beyond that twilight and even in the midst of that pitiful cry there seemed to dawn a ray of light and to sound a note not wholly of despair. (Butler, 1892, pp. 97–98)

In her life there was to be a deep engagement with the world of twilight, where darkness and light meet. Here she felt a sense of hope, a desire to be with and for women, and an awareness of being called towards heaven and away from the forces which seem to push people down to hell. She was to display a particular concern for those women whose experience of life was that of being pushed down to hell. It was in this area of concern that she was to devise new ways of an inclusive Church acting as prophetic leaven in a corrupt society.

In 1852 she married George Butler and they went to live in Oxford, where she was horrified by the male, misogynist atmosphere. She had three children in the space of five years and was not well in the damp climate of the Thames valley. In 1857, when she was expecting her fourth child, the family moved to enable George to become Vice-Principal of Cheltenham College.

In 1864 tragedy struck. George and Josephine returned home one evening from a social function. Their six-year-old daughter Eva rushed out of her room upstairs to greet them. She leaned too far over the banisters and crashed down to her death on the stone floor at their feet below. As a young woman Josephine Butler had had a vision of a cry, the pain, wanting to respond and finding hope in despair. Now she encountered a deep experience of such emotions, quite literally in the fall of this very young female.

Understandably she suffered from depression. During the next years she consulted nine male doctors, who each advised rest and quiet, a prescription which illustrates the Victorian male view of women. Because this advice was not helping, she eventually consulted the first British woman doctor, Miss Garrett, who gave her a very different perspective. She advised that Josephine would get well through strenuous work, not through rest. This advice proved to be very accurate and provides another pointer to Josephine Butler's spirituality, which was always more than resting in words. It was rooted in the vision that active engagement is essential to wholeness of life.

At the time of their bereavement, the Butlers used the following prayer: 'O God look upon the earth, its sins, its sorrows, its wrongs: Give us patience to wait and watch for the dawn of blessing as those who watch for the morning' (Butler, 1892, p. 155). Here we have the key ingredients of Josephine Butler's understanding of Christian faith and life: that God offers goodness, which can be trusted; that this life is marred by sin, sorrow, wrong; and that our primary response should be the prayer which lays these perplexities before God and trusts in the promise of forgiveness, healing and new life. It is in this way that we learn to acknowledge our need of God, which comes before our more human needs of understanding and comfort. From this discipline of waiting and watching comes fresh vision and energy to strive for God's Kingdom as bringing in a new day. Such a process happens in *God's time*, within the prospect of eternity.

EXERCISE

How does this holding together of human frailty, prayer, God's graciousness and further commissions for the Kingdom relate to Herbert's understanding of a *parochial* spirituality?

Evangelical energy: women and the family

Two factors provide an important background to Josephine Butler's subsequent career. The first is the place of the family in Victorian culture. As the public world became increasingly secular in its ethos, despite the trappings of established religion, so religion became a matter of private choice. This was a process enhanced by both the catholic and the evangelical revivals, with their appeals to people to join and participate in essentially voluntary societies. In terms of Anglican theology, the connection between these two worlds of public secularity and private religiousness was made by the parochial system, which provided a common context as in Herbert's model.

However, in practice the parish church had little contact with much of the population and the *de facto* connector of public and private worlds became the *family*. Here was the place where those who exercised power in the world, that is to say *men* in Victorian times, found nurture, support and formation, largely through the moral influences of women. This factor is basic to the 'two spheres' understanding of men and women so prevalent in the nineteenth century. Josephine Butler was significant in recognising that the family was an essential unit for Church and society, a key tool in the revival of a parochial spirituality and a properly national Church. And yet she was able to press for significant changes in the roles and relationships of men and women within this God-given framework.

Second, it was the evangelical revival which, through the example of people such as Hannah More, began to provide opportunities for women to assume significant public roles outside the sphere of the home. Clearly the industrial revolution provided the chance for women to work outside their home and their very local community, in the much more impersonal and public world of factories and mines. However, the development of more positive public roles for women came from their involvement in religious revival. This began by extending the traditional domestic role: visiting other women to deliver tracts, offering pastoral care and teaching literacy and hygiene. This soon led to women taking leading roles in campaigns for social welfare and political change.

Josephine Butler is a key icon in this shift – both in her own story, and in her particular concern for the rights and opportunities of women.

EXERCISE

Does the family still have a significant role in forging the identity of a parochial Church?

To what extent have women now achieved access to exercising their gifts in public life?

Prayer becomes prophetic and political

In 1866 George Butler moved to become Principal of Liverpool College. In Liverpool Josephine Butler began her work with prostitutes, a ministry for which she is famous. In the city at that time there were some 9,000 prostitutes, many only thirteen or fourteen years old. One of the few ways in which such girls could earn what they called 'untainted pence' was to pick oakum (loose fibres from old ropes). Josephine Butler began to go and pick oakum with some of these girls. She arrived smartly dressed and initially suffered a fair amount of scorn. She persevered, however.

Another feature of her approach is the constant interaction of prayer and pastoral contact. As she came to know the girls, she used to pray with them. She recalled a girl who recited the fourteenth chapter of John's gospel, with the text 'my peace I leave with you.' This girl could not read, but she had learned this wonderful passage about hope and care. Josephine Butler records that she said to the girls:

> Now let us kneel and cry to that same Jesus who spoke these words. And down on their knees they fell every one of them, reverently on that damp stone floor, some saying the words after me – the Lord's Prayer – others moaning and weeping. It is a strange sound that united wail, like a great murmur of vague desire and hope issuing from the heart of despair, piercing the gloom and the murky atmosphere of that vaulted room and reaching to the heart of God. (Butler, 1892, p. 184)

Here was Josephine Butler praying with others, in their need, as they offered inarticulate protest about being pulled down to hell and desiring heaven. This is prayer and pastoral contact intertwined.

In this example we see the prayers of Josephine Butler and of these girls becoming public and shared. Although the prayers are vague, they are full of power and a sense of purpose. Those praying, as in her earlier vision, did not know where they wanted to go, but they wanted to go somewhere. And even in such an apparently hopeless situation there is hope. Praying brings all these people and all these factors together to give a sense of purpose, hope and forward movement. This is a model Josephine develops with great force. It is the practical expression of Laud's theology of re-formation.

Before long she was using her home as a refuge for fallen women, especially for those who were too ill to work as prostitutes, sometimes too diseased or sick with consumption, often starving. George would always meet a new arrival at the door and take them on his arm to their room. They were welcomed as an honoured guest. Josephine Butler's vision had included a notion of refuge.

Because of George's position as Principal of Liverpool College they were well connected and Josephine persuaded wealthy people to contribute funds for the work, and doctors to provide a free service. This model of involving others in her work through their money and power and skills is another basic ingredient of her later life. It also provides a key insight into her approach to the Christian life in a hostile world.

In summary, we may note a number of different ingredients in her approach. There is the sense of a call to help people in need: those who are struggling to reverse being drawn into hell, and who aspire to heaven. There is a recognition of her own pain and suffering and struggle (we cannot pray for others and desire to help them unless we have learned to recognise something of our own pains and struggle) and the importance of actually being alongside those in need as they are being pushed towards hell.

She also expresses a spirituality that embraces an intertwining of prayer and pastoral care which leads to a practical response (some kind of refuge is offered). In her life prayer and care issues into something practical. She involves others who are not directly in contact with the needy but who can become part of this incarnational work and witness through contributing their prayers, money and talents. Her spirituality includes an element of prayer as reflection. Josephine did not simply pray that these women would be saved and healed and receive a roof over their heads. Her prayer involved reflection on the possible causes of their plight and ways of responding to it. Thus her prayer led to the exercise of a political judgement. She said that economics lie at the very root of practical morality. Prostitution was an economic problem; it is because of economics that women are driven into prostitution. For Josephine Butler, political judgement is important. To listen to the prayers of needy people and to pray with them and share their concerns will lead to political concerns. Part of God's will is done through political and social processes.

Throughout all these ingredients, Christ is the great guide and template. Josephine Butler often spoke of Jesus' pity towards women and his anger at man's injustice. She wrote the following words to a prostitute about to give birth to an illegitimate child:

> You remember how sweet and lovely Jesus always was to women, and how he helped their woman diseases and how respectful He was to them and loved them and forgave the sins of the most sinful. And He was born of a woman, a woman only. No man had any hand in that. It was such an honour to women. (Butler, 1954, pp. 58–59)

EXERCISE

Look again at the ingredients of Josephine Butler's approach to spirituality, as outlined in the preceding section.

How do they relate to your own ideas, especially about prayer?

How might they form a basis for prophecy (right words) and politics (right action)?

Beyond parochialism: the national Church is crucial

From 1864 Josephine Butler was a key person in a campaign against the Contagious Diseases Acts. This legislation was enacted in the 1860s in response to the problem of venereal disease, then becoming prevalent among the troops in certain garrison towns. Soldiers were the heroes of nineteenth-century Britain as the spearhead of the spread of the Empire. They needed protection from this outbreak of disease, which is why the government made laws that meant that in certain garrison towns any woman who was suspected of being a prostitute could be arrested, forcibly examined and, if necessary, forcibly treated.

Josephine Butler became a key figure in a campaign calling for the repeal of this legislation. She achieved enormous notoriety, partly because of the subject matter which was not thought suitable for a Victorian lady, partly because many people opposed women exercising any sort of leadership role, and partly because the action was seen to be anti-establishment. Many leading churchmen thought that the legislation was an eminently sensible way of controlling the disease.

Her opposition was based on three major points.

1. The laws infringed the rights of women, who should be free to walk in their own town without fear of arrest and possible examination.
2. The law had the effect of legalising prostitution, and simply established ways of trying to control some of its possible effects.
3. No blame was attached to men, the aim was simply to protect them. Fault and remedial action lie solely with women.

The battle to repeal these Acts raged until 1886. For twenty years Josephine Butler was at the heart of a tireless campaign. She frequently visited other European countries to help organise protests against similar legislation. She met great hostility, being attacked, pelted and once having an upstairs meeting room set on fire while she was speaking. Her opponents included many church people.

She came to realise that women had to rely upon themselves. Generally, the only men who would help seemed to be working-class men. There were, of course, noble exceptions among her peer group. The methods of the campaign were meetings, speeches, petitions, letter-writing and pressure in Parliament. For Josephine Butler all these activities were accompanied by prayer – both deep personal prayer and public prayer meetings that she called to support the various activities of the campaign. When Parliament debated the issues, she helped to organise a great series of prayer meetings involving campaigners, Members of Parliament and friendly supporters, with centres right across the country. People were invited to drop in and offer their prayer support as a key way of registering a political commitment regarding this area of concern.

We can trace here the key elements of:

- personal concern – expressed in prayer and then in action;
- engagement with those in need, who provide the key perspective – the agenda for prophetic action;
- encouraging support from church people and others of good will;
- crystallising political aims and a strategy to fulfil them (including the international dimension);
- confronting opposition and apathy;

- proclaiming an alternative Gospel and political programme;
- persevering, often against seemingly hopeless odds, both in prayer and in campaigning;
- witnessing to every advance by giving thanks to God in an act of public worship.

We can see Josephine Butler identifying an agenda for the Church in English culture that was determined by desperate human need, at a time when the energy of many Christian leaders was focused on issues such as the institutional reform of the Church, biblical criticism and scientific challenges to traditional apologetics. Each of these other issues had the effect of drawing people more deeply within the voluntary institution, hoping that in making it more perfect a more effective witness might be given. In fact none of these issues had this effect. They were rather the cause of increasing division and disarray.

By contrast, Josephine Butler saw that the Church had an essential role in the nation as salt and leaven. She therefore worked with others for practical issues about the grace and dignity of all human beings: men, women and children. This is an important model for the working of the parish system at a more local level.

Here is a witness to Anglican inclusivity which takes seriously the role of a distinctive Christianity (Gore), is focused in small local groups (Herbert, Law) that must be joined to uphold catholic principles that apply to everyone (Hooker, Laud), working with all people of goodwill at addressing the common problems of humanity (Joseph Butler). For Josephine Butler this enterprise requires rooting in prayer, personal and public; recognised leadership; identification with those most in need and ecumenical co-operation.

This style of Christian witness was mirrored by many other campaigns for justice and wholeness in the nineteenth century, with the formative model being the campaign against the slave trade. It was exemplified in the work of Church leaders such as Bishop Samuel Wilberforce, who began to organise dioceses according to similar principles, uniting evangelical energy (the power of the Gospel) with a commitment to catholic principles (those necessary for all people). Moves towards the revival of Convocation and the eventual development of a synodical system of government in the Church of England have been similarly influenced by this way of understanding the role and function of a national Church, with a continuing tension between the inward pull of the institution's own agenda and the external demands of human frailty and perplexities.

EXERCISE

Is Josephine Butler's way of working a realistic model for how a national Church might operate in a secular culture?

How can the Church resist the temptation to concentrate on its own imperfections and thus engage more fully with the needs of the wider community?

What are the implications of Josephine Butler's model for the parochial system and for synodical government?

Prayer and national responsibilities

Josephine Butler was clear that human society is the place where the drama of salvation is enacted. The Church is witness to this reality.

> Through prayer we open ourselves to God's creative activity in human affairs . . . In holding to God, you and He together hold and would wield a vast energy and power . . . The day is coming when we shall be astonished and ashamed to think that for so many centuries the power possible to man has been limited or denied by the narrowness of human conceptions and the elementary state of our knowledge . . . He has been showing me that beyond His promises and beyond scripture He Himself is God, and that His character is our great eternal hope and confidence . . . God is all powerful but at the same time dependent on man's ability to respond. (Butler, 1954, p. 179)

In a similar vein she wrote:

> Looking at any of the great questions before us now – the relations of nation to nation, and of the Anglo-Saxon race to the heathen populations of conquered countries; questions of gold-seeking, of industry, of capital and labour, of the influence of wealth, now so great a power in our country and its dependencies; questions of legal enactments, of the action of Governments, and innumerable social and economic problems – we may ask, how much of the light of heaven is permitted to fall on those questions? How many or how few are there among us who ask, and seek, and knock and wait, to know *God's* thoughts on these matters? (Johnson, 1909, p. 238)

Thus the Church existed to provide appropriate places and forums for prayer – as the focus for recognising human need, the offer of God's grace and the possibilities of concrete action for the Kingdom.

In an increasingly complex and interdependent world, there was a key role for the Church to act in this way at a national level, both as part of the establishment in English culture and also ecumenically. Moreover, this role must relate to international considerations and connections. Josephine Butler's story provides an example of how this challenge could be taken up in a way that owned the inclusiveness of the Anglican tradition while adjusting to a secular and indifferent world.

EXERCISE

How can Christian aspirations today be raised from local concerns towards the national and international issues that so influence human being?

What do you think are the advantages and disadvantages of establishment for the Church of England?

📖 **Read Acts 8:26–40.** How can the practice of prayer be a means of challenging and changing others? You might like to consider:
- 'an angel of the Lord said to Philip', who was clearly attentive to God;
- the Ethiopian was a Gentile, an outsider, but desired to worship God;
- he was best met in the space between his usual world and his desire for a deeper knowledge of God enacted in his pilgrimage. Between the two extremes is the possibility of deep encounter;
- Scripture is a key resource;
- Scripture and the Ethiopian's experience both need interpretation by someone appointed to this task;
- the crucial encounter takes place in the carriage, while both were journeying, seeking to go further;
- the focus is the crucified and risen Messiah;
- baptism is the sign of challenge and change: identification with the catholic institution of the Church through its officer; ▶▶

- the miracle of the Holy Spirit is administered;
- prayer has been answered, both people have been changed;
- two different cultures have been reconciled in God's greater purposes for human kind.

Further reading

Bell, E (1962), *Josephine Butler: flame of fire*, London, Constable.

Boyd, N (1982), *Josephine Butler, Octavia Hill, Florence Nightingale*, London, Macmillan.

Butler, A S G (1954), *Portrait of Josephine Butler*, London, Faber and Faber.

Butler, J (1892), *Recollections of George Butler*, Bristol, Arrowsmith.

Butler, J (1896), *Personal Reminiscences of a Great Crusade*, London, Horace Marshall.

Fawcett, M G and Turner, E M (1927), *Josephine Butler*, London, The Association for Moral and Social Hygiene.

Gore, C (1916), *The Religion of the Church*, London, Mowbray.

Johnson, G W and Johnson, L A (eds) (1909), *Josephine E Butler: an autobiographical memoir*, London, Arrowsmith.

Petrie, G (1971), *A Singular Iniquity*, London, Macmillan.

Purcell, W (1988), *Anglican Spirituality: a continuing tradition*, London, Mowbray.

9. PAROCHIALISM REALIGNED

Introduction

The development of new models for being an established Church needed to be paralleled by a re-formation of the parochial system. The issue was most acute in the teeming slums of major cities, where parochial identity and community awareness were almost non-existent. Local loyalties survived, but with little relationship to any notion of Church or of the responsibilities of neighbourhood. This undermining of the traditional parish system spread steadily in the twentieth century, from urban to suburban areas, eventually into the heart of rural life. People formed significant relationships through networks that were other than geographic.

A creative response to this situation can be seen in the work of Henrietta Barnett, both in helping forge appropriate connections between the local and the wider contexts (for the Church and for the wider community) and in establishing an imaginative parochial framework to encourage and support a sense of place and belonging among modern citizens.

Reflecting on experience
In what sense can you describe the people among whom you live as 'neighbours'? How does this relate to a Christian understanding of 'neighbour'?

If there are differences, to what might they be attributed? ▶▶

EXERCISE
📖 **Read Acts 9:1–19.** The violence of the outsider is converted to committed membership. You might like to consider:

- Saul, the person who is assumed to be 'enlightened', is given a new light;
- his original vision disappears, he becomes blind to old perspectives;
- he needs to receive help and encouragement from a Christian believer;
- he is praying for help;
- Ananias is *sent* to this person in his own neighbourhood;
- he must risk going to the place of opposition and apparent incompatibility;
- Saul's eyes are opened – scales fall from them. Now he connects with the Gospel, is baptised and filled with the Holy Spirit;
- Saul's companions are not mentioned – what happens to them?
- there is an important dynamic between what happens on the journey (coming from outside) and what happens in the place of dwelling (inside the place that is home).

Henrietta Barnett (1851–1936)

She was born Henrietta Rowland and married Samuel Barnett when she was twenty-two years old. They went to live and work in the parish of St Jude's Whitechapel in East London, an area of enormous poverty and deprivation. Samuel was appointed vicar. Three stories about Henrietta can set the scene for understanding her contribution to the development of Anglican tradition and the parochial system.

The first concerns her work in Whitechapel. Inevitably she became involved in schemes to try and meet the physical needs of the people, particularly by supplying food and clothing. However, she devoted a great deal of time and energy to organising concerts in the church. She persuaded famous performers and musicians to come from the West End to sing and make music in St Jude's, and in an age before television or radio the parishioners came in great numbers. Henrietta also began to organise art exhibitions in the church. In the long run this activity led to the establishment of the Whitechapel Art Gallery. Once again she persuaded artists and wealthy owners of works of art to loan paintings for free exhibitions. Henrietta was convinced that it was important to touch people's minds and imaginations as well as to care for their bodies.

The second story concerns the key role she played in the creation of what became the Hampstead Garden Suburb. This was a scheme to rehouse people from some of the dreadful slum areas in the centre of London, and one of Henrietta's prime concerns was that every family should have its own space and its own garden in order to find a proper sense of identity. This was in reaction to her own experience in Whitechapel where whole families lived in one room. Community facilities were also provided in the Garden Suburb, for she knew that it was important to bring people together. She wrote of the Garden Suburb scheme:

> It grew out of my realisation that different social classes suffered from their ignorance of each other. For all the rich to live in one quarter of the town, and for all the poor to be grouped together in another robs each section of the pleasure of each other's friendship and the development of character and the enlargement of interests which naturally follow. The Hampstead Garden Suburb was planned so that persons of many standards of income should be able to live in neighbourliness. (Barnett, 1918, p. 324)

The third story recalls the herculean efforts Henrietta made organising trips into the countryside for those trapped in the slums of East London. She wanted to help them experience something of the glory of Nature: to see God's own living handiwork in woods and plants, in fields and streams. And true to her entrepreneurial style she involved all kinds of friends and contacts in this work. One result was that people began to see the importance of preserving the beautiful countryside near London that was within reach of the poor. Ultimately these endeavours led to the foundation of the National Trust, to preserve Nature and its beauty for ordinary people.

These three stories are deeply prophetic and symbolic for her contribution to Anglican identity and the reshaping of parochial spirituality. It is important to recall that her life spans the shift from a confident age of Christian vitality and moral certitude, to an inter-war period of uncertainty and questioning. Henrietta lived through a period in which modern awareness of secularism and pluralism became much clearer, and in her life and work she offers important clues to recalling Anglicanism to a tradition that was formed amid competing views and in a hostile secular environment.

EXERCISE
Reflect on these stories as providing a strategy for the parish system.

The role of the Church: from monologue to dialogue to ...?

For centuries in English religious culture, our understanding of the role of the Church has been based upon a 'Christendom mentality'. This is the great medieval picture of a Church that oversees the whole of human life and exercises control over law, morality, education and social life. This was reinforced in England at the Reformation by the formation of an established Church which claimed a monopoly, and thus tended to offer a 'monologue' to the society in which it is set. Increasingly this monopoly has been challenged and undermined by the growth of other denominations and by the development of non-Christian ways of understanding and organising human life.

One of the responses of the Church of England has been to acknowledge the loss of its 'monologue relationship' to society, and to understand itself more in terms of dialogue. The Church stands for the Gospel. The world needs the Gospel. The missionary strategy is one of engagement between Church and world. This approach resonates with some of the dimensions of the evangelical and catholic movements of revival.

However, this has proved to be an over-optimistic analysis. The Church of England has become increasingly marginal. It is of no real account in the life of the nation or in the life of the great majority of its citizens. It is no longer a major player in the significant dialogues in our society. It still has the trappings of power – bishops are allowed to let off steam in the House of Lords – but by no stretch of the imagination could it be said that the Church of England is a major force in the key dialogues in our society. This is why so much of its energy is being put into the organisation of its own life: at least the Church can take itself seriously, even if no one else does!

Moreover, religion has become private, voluntary, domestic and dualistic. Most religious people keep their religiousness to themselves and their 'private' life. When they are in public roles, there is little way of knowing whether people are religious or not. There is a strong dualism in the experience and practice of religion in contemporary society.

The major problem with the notion of dialogue is that it has generally been advanced on the assumption that the Church has a monopoly of the Gospel. The Church is often seen to 'hold the Gospel' and needs to deliver it to those outside. This has never been the view of Anglicanism, as Hooker and Laud made clear in their teaching that the whole of creation is full of God-given potential struggling to find its appropriate form. Bishop Butler offered a similar insight into the important but partial role of the Church in the struggle of created life to know and honour its creator. There is a dynamic that allows all God's creation to contribute, and yet there is a key role for a minority Church. Butler and Gore advanced an understanding of this truth; Henrietta Barnett offers a more practical example of how Christian life might be lived, and Church life might be ordered, to take account of this profound reality that has always been fundamental to the Anglican tradition.

EXERCISE

Can you argue a case for the importance of either monologue or dialogue as the proper mode of relationship between Church and world?

What does this imply for the parish system? Are there alternative approaches?

Some lessons from the work of Henrietta Barnett

From the stories used to illustrate her work we can gain a number of important clues. It is important to remember that it was not just Henrietta Barnett doing those things – it was the local Church, within which she was a major source of energy! From these stories we may note that:

• Christian believing is not private;
• Christian believing demands participation in the life of the local Church – common worship and common witness;
• Christian believing demands participation in the life of the local community through the local Church;
• Christian believing involves a common striving of different groups and classes in a combined effort to combat human need as a sign of the possibilities of the Kingdom.

It was the Church in Whitechapel that provided a place for Christians to co-operate in offering facilities for concerts and exhibitions, inviting partnership between rich and poor, making connections within the community and honouring a desire for each family to have space to know themselves and the goodness of creation. In an address in 1922, Barnett proclaimed that those who would help the needy should 'copy the plan adopted by God the Father': 'To share our best possessions – be they art, music, literature, thought, knowledge, friends, happiness, beauty, ideals, hope; to share, not to stand on a platform and shower down, but to stand on the floor and share, shoulder to shoulder.' And also 'to create fellowship, which links, binds, enlarges, deepens, gladdens, saddens, halves sorrows and doubles joys' (Barnett, 1930, p. 62).

Perhaps the best known example of this approach is in the work that she undertook with her husband in the University Settlement Movement. The Barnetts went to Oxford and appealed to students to come to the East End when they left the University. They built a 'college-like' structure called Toynbee Hall, where young people came to live in the East End for several years, pursuing professional training and careers in the city but spending evenings and weekends helping the local Church to offer all kinds of activities and opportunities to the community – from boxing classes to literacy. All these activities helped to enrich and educate the local Church, the local community and the young people concerned.

EXERCISE

Henrietta Barnett saw the parish as the place for bringing together Christian witness, something of the variety of God's gifts and human need. To what extent could this vision simply be a way of preserving the status quo?

The re-formation of a parochial Church

Reflecting upon this brief introduction to Barnett's theological rationale and parochial practice (which was offered alongside and as part of her husband's work as the vicar), we note that the scheme of parish activities – for example concerts, exhibitions, nature walks, Garden Suburbs – does not provide an overtly Christian agenda. Church members were rooted in common worship but their parochial activities were only 'implicitly Christian'. There is always an invitation to members of the parish to join the Christian fellowship but in practice what is most clearly on offer is participation in a set of social activities. There is an engagement with physical need: the Church offered food and clothing supplies, but people's deepest needs are more than physical. The key task is to touch and feed the soul.

Henrietta Barnett realised this too and sought to fulfil it through the method of 'glimpses'. She knew that most human beings, including Christians, have glimpses of God. Few people consciously live in a fully worked-out and systematic theological scheme. She was very realistic! Only a few people move beyond 'glimpses' of God to a more articulated, systematic and self-conscious Christian belief and practice. These 'few' are those Gore talks about as being 'moulded'. But all of God's creatures can and do know something of glory, goodness, beauty, truth and the call to eternity. But this is met in moments, episodically: through being moved at a concert, or standing in front of a painting, or going for a walk and seeing a flower. For Henrietta that was natural and acceptable. It is vital to encourage these things so as to help each of us fight against the darker side of us which so often predominates, the forces which pull us down into the hell of selfishness and greed.

Of her concerts she wrote in 1882: 'To trace the result is impossible, and not advisable; but who can doubt that in those moments, brief as they were, the curtain of the flesh was raised and the soul became visible, perhaps by the discovery startling its possessor into new aspirations?' (Barnett and Barnett, 1894, p. 94).

The Church's task is to provide opportunities for those moments which light and feed the soul. This is spirituality properly understood. Sometimes people will seek fuller interpretation and exploration, but generally we need to be ever engaged with 'moments' in which we can glimpse a sense of glory and the hope of something more. The life of God is known in those things. John's gospel is the most profound witness to the truth that God is known in the ordinary things of life if we can learn to see them properly: in bread and wine, in wedding parties and in a woman caught in adultery. All such things can bear grace if we learn to see them properly: to glimpse the hope and glory and graciousness of God and of his love in them.

Of her nature walks she added, 'For people spending long years in the close courts and streets of ugly towns, the mere sight of Nature is startling, and may awaken longings, to themselves strange and indescribable but which are the stirrings of the life within' (Barnett and Barnett, 1894, p. 95). Henrietta Barnett's concerts, exhibitions and nature walks gave such glimpses, and they gave them to people *in fellowship*. People were not called to have just a private, individual experience. Their glimpsing was part of a corporate activity. Learning to see is always linked to learning to be in fellowship, in communion.

People need a sense of place in order properly to discover their own identity. This is true for families and also for friendship. Henrietta campaigned for such 'space' for people at a time when mission was focused on church building and church space. Spirituality operates domestically as well as ecclesiastically. A parish acknowledges both facts.

EXERCISE

How do you respond to Henrietta Barnett's understanding of human and Christian spirituality?

What might be missing in her conception of the task of the Church?

The re-formation of a parochial spirituality

This notion of the role of the parish Church provides a number of insights that clarify issues regarding the unfolding of the Anglican tradition in our own times.

The Church no longer offers a monologue to society: a single theological and moral system and an all-embracing institution. The opportunity for serious dialogue is limited. Yet the Church has a vital role in acknowledging that grace comes from outside, in glimpses. God is known as a mysterious power and purpose who breaks into the world, often through human creativity, fellowship and the beauty of the world (Joseph Butler).

Similarly, the Church holds the reality of the Messiah and the miracle of the presence of the Holy Spirit as giving such glimpses deeper meaning and connection. There is always further evidence (Laud) to be tested and embraced by the 'mould' of the Gospel given to the Church (Gore). Common worship gives rhythm and focus to this way of knowing God (Herbert). Christian mission and witness is to call others to this rhythm of worship. St Jude's Whitechapel organised concerts, exhibitions and outings. Most of the world live by what we might call 'secular liturgy' and 'secular spirituality': rarely, if ever, coming to Church worship but exploring the same agenda through 'glimpses' – occasions for eyes to be opened and new hopes embraced – enriched by a context of fellowship. This effect is recognised in recent times by a growing desire for 'new' occasional offices, to mark significant moments in human lives. In this sense the local Church can be self-consciously and contentedly a minority: recognising the importance of its own distinctive worship, creeds, moral and social life (Gore).

The appropriate strategy is neither a monologue nor a dialogue, but the much more gentle task of trying to engage anyone and everyone with those things central to the Gospel – learning to see truth, beauty, goodness, justice, forgiveness and hopefulness, and thus being inspired towards eternity and the fulfilment of these things. This is the meaning of incarnation: the life of God enfleshed for a moment, in a particular place, as beauty and grace meet us amidst suffering, struggle and all the trappings of human mortality. More, this is the meaning of atonement: being made one with God in losing the self in some greater whole. The sign of the crucified giving up his life in a moment is the germ of resurrection and a model of all that can lift us up from human failing and limitation.

Hence the proper task of the Church in a place is that of the remnant, inviting others to join but recognising that in the mystery of God's way of working in this world most of his children will best respond to participation in secular liturgy and secular spirituality. This is why church fetes and car boot sales are as important elements of mission for the Anglican tradition as high mass and guest Alpha services. Anglicanism exists in the eye of the believer.

EXERCISE

Try to develop a case for the value of church fetes and car boot sales in the enfleshing of a properly parochial spirituality.

The place of participation

Hooker called for ever-clearer participation in Christ, through the life of his Church. Barnett developed a way of seeking to honour that approach in a non-Christian culture. Two other processes have attempted to enflesh this vision of participation.

Democracy has been a relatively recent attempt in terms of political organisation to acknowledge the uniqueness of each person while providing a framework for co-operation and a commonly acknowledged system of authority. It may be that the bankruptcy of this process is becoming evident as we recognise an increasing concern with rights and the neglect of duties, the failure to provide adequate connection between the local and the national, the difficulties in creating a sense of commonalty between people in a given area and the cynical manipulation of the system by political and commercial forces.

The media-communications culture claims to provide sophisticated connection between individuals, ideas and institutions. Again there is no real commitment to promoting any sense of place, or of belonging alongside others as neighbours. It may be that a parochial culture which is part of a national Church, in the ways explored in relation to Charles Gore and Henrietta Barnett, could provide a more attractive possibility for the kind of participation which is both theologically and socially desirable.

Barnett was concerned to create an atmosphere of opportunity – in rural walking, works of art and concerts, focused in a particular place. For her, Christian mission is much more than words and is more effectively rooted in art galleries and country walks than in books and sermons. This accords with the insights of the Anglican tradition which we have been exploring, where the focus is on the local and the small scale: centred on a remnant reaching out to a wider world and calling people to share glimpses of the God who comes to all his children, Christians and non-Christians alike. The mystery of incarnation and atonement, coming from beyond into our souls, is focused in Messiah and miracles for the few; but it is real and profound for everyone else also.

EXERCISE
What kind of participation is demanded by the Christian Gospel and how might it best be ordered?

Implications for being a parish

These insights show us the nature of a parish in the Anglican tradition, as we have explored it.

1. It would be a place where there is a Christian remnant with a distinctive, collegial life. Joseph Butler and Charles Gore emphasise the centrality of Messiah and miracles, and of working together at creed, worship, moral life and social life in ways that 'mould' a distinctive and character-forming witness and message to others. Common worship is foundational.

2. It would be a place where there will be a Christian community that

goes on seeking truth through exploration, through 'comparing independent testimonies' (Gore) and through 'further evidence' (Laud): a Christian community that seeks to go on growing.

3. It would be a place where there is invitation and a call from the Christian group to anybody else to join it and its explorations.
4. It would be a place where there is openness to God coming from beyond to touch and enlighten souls, minds and bodies.
5. It would be a place where the spirituality of the Church and of the non-Church is episodic, unsystematic, tailored to moments of richness, open to further evidence, trusting in giving people freedom and space to live their lives. Church and non-Church have a common spirituality.
6. It would be a place where the Church group allows the world to live by its own secular liturgies and spiritualities, with its own way of opening eyes to uncover the glory and greatness and truth of God. Christians can rejoice in these things.
7. It would be a place where there is a dynamic between the Christian remnant and others *that is necessary for both*. Both are open to a God who comes from beyond.
8. It would be a place where the Church group interacts with the non-Church *on the world's terms*, through going on walks, looking at pictures, hearing lovely music. Different areas will have different ways of appropriately inviting people to open their eyes. The Church will clearly base its participation in such activities on its witness to what Joseph Butler calls Messiah and miracles – those key moments and events that allow Christians to interpret the glimpses of glory. However the Church will not impose these things on others. It will start with allowing secular liturgy, such as walks and concerts, to be places of revelation – though always inviting others to move further on in the search for glory.

EXERCISE

What would you add or subtract from these features of being a parish?

How does this way of thinking relate to your initial reflections about a Christian understanding of 'neighbour'? ▶▶

   📖 **Read Acts 9:20–43.** What might these stories say about the life
and witness of the local Church? You might like to consider:
- Paul, called to be an apostle, visits Churches which are located in a number of places;
- each place has its own concerns;
- there is a clear distinction between believers and non-believers, which it is important to address;
- Paul is accepted as an apostle because he is a witness to the resurrection of Jesus;
- effective mission comes not through proclamation and argument (Paul in Damascus and Jerusalem) but in engaging with human need and mortality (Peter with Aeneas and Tabitha);
- the most powerful sign of new life comes through one who made shirts and coats for others;
- when Peter attends to human need and frailty the response is moments of enlightenment, which become formational experiences for those concerned.

Further reading

Barnett, H (1918), *Canon Barnett*, London, John Murray.

Barnett, H (1930), *Matters that Matter*, London, John Murray.

Barnett, S A and H (1915), *Practicable Socialism*, London, Longmans, Green.

Chadwick, O (1970), *The Victorian Church*, two volumes, London, A and C Black.

Ecclestone, G (ed.) (1988), *The Parish Church?* Oxford, Mowbray.

Gilbert, A D (1980), *The Making of Post-Christian Britain*, London, Longman.

Hempton, D (1996), *Religion and Political Culture in Britain and Ireland*, Cambridge, Cambridge University Press.

Knight, F (1995), *The Nineteenth-Century Church and English Society*, Cambridge, Cambridge University Press.

10. ANGLICANISM WORLDWIDE

Introduction

As English political and commercial interests spread across the globe Anglicanism soon followed, and by the end of the twentieth century the Anglican Communion had become a worldwide family of autonomous Churches.

In this chapter we will trace the outline of this development and examine its implications for the Anglican tradition, using some of the insights of Michael Ramsey who was one of the first truly international Archbishops of Canterbury, travelling extensively to visit different parts of the Communion.

Reflecting on experience

Make a list of six of the main differences there might be between living in a small African village and in a large American city.

What can you learn from this exercise about the relationship between different cultures?

EXERCISE

📖 **Read Acts 10.** What does this story tell us about Christianity in different cultures? You might like to consider the following points.

- The Gentile Cornelius had a rich spirituality but sought something more.
- Peter, despite his Jewish upbringing, was content to stay in the home of a leather-worker, who was involved in an unclean trade.
- Peter was tempted to keep his religion separate from his actual context. ▶▶

> - New insights come from the discipline of prayer ('the ninth hour', 'the sixth hour').
> - Peter travels to the Gentile's home.
> - He takes companions with him.
> - God is already present, particularly in the works of charity of Cornelius.
> - 'Whoever worships God, and does what is right is acceptable to him, no matter what race he belongs to' (v. 35).
> - Peter shares the story of Jesus of Nazareth, living, dying and rising, as a fulfilment of Scripture.
> - The Holy Spirit blesses the Gentiles.
> - The task of Peter and his companions is to respond by offering baptism.
> - They stayed with them for a few days, for the new relationship in the common faith needs consolidating.

Michael Ramsey (1904–1988)

Michael Ramsey was both an academic and a priest. He worked in parishes in Liverpool and Boston (Lincolnshire), he was a teacher at Lincoln Theological College and professor of theology at Durham and Cambridge Universities. Then he became successively Bishop of Durham, Archbishop of York and, in 1961, the one hundredth Archbishop of Canterbury.

Geoffrey Fisher, his predecessor, was the first Archbishop of Canterbury to use air-travel to visit many of the provinces and dioceses of the Anglican Communion 'to encourage, and bless, and discover what was happening, and foster the links between the mother church of Canterbury and its now very numerous and very various children' (Chadwick, 1990, p. 209).

Ramsey took up this part of his responsibilities with relish and to great effect. As a theologian, Ramsey was deeply influenced by the inclusive tradition articulated by Richard Hooker, F D Maurice and Charles Gore. In an article entitled 'What is Anglican Theology?', he wrote:

> The method, use, and direction characteristic of Anglican divinity first came into clear light in the writings of Hooker. His theology claimed to do both far less and far more than the theologies of Calvin, of Luther, and of Trent. It did less in that it eschewed any attempt to offer

a complete scheme of biblical doctrine, or an experiential assurance of justification, or an infallible system of dogma. It did more in that it appealed to a larger field of authority and dealt with the whole person rather than with certain parts of him or her. For it appealed to scripture, tradition, and reason: 'the Spirit everywhere in the scripture . . . laboureth to confirm us in the things which we believe by things whereof we have sensible knowledge.' And it dealt with the whole person, both by its reverence for reason and conscience and by its refusal to draw a circle around the inward personal element in religion and to separate it from the world of external things. It was congruous with all this that the incarnation, with the doctrine of the two natures, was central, and that the church and the sacraments were closely linked with the incarnation. The claim of this theology to be 'Catholic' rested not only upon its affinity with antiquity but upon the true 'wholeness' of its authorities and of its treatment of human beings and their need. It offered them not only justification in their inward self but the sanctification of their whole being through sharing in the divine life. (Ramsey, 1945, pp. 2–3)

We may note the emphasis upon the whole person, the refusal to separate the inward personal element in religion from the world of external things, the fact that 'catholic' means 'wholeness' in the treatment of human beings and their need, and the calling for sanctification of their whole being through sharing in the divine life.

EXERCISE
Can you identify connections with other Anglican thinkers mentioned in this book?

Ramsey claimed this bedrock of Anglican tradition as the basis for dealing with a world in which the Church was increasingly marginal, where there were complex debates about morality, politics, sexuality, nationalism and colonialism; and global interdependence was becoming a clearer reality for many people. His approach may be gauged from two addresses. The first was given in Lincoln (England).

See what manner of stones are here, in this lovely Minster of Lincoln. See too what manner of men and women. May we before we go home today picture to ourselves what Christ's spiritual house might be, fulfilling the dreams of the old missionaries of this land. I see a community of Christians conscious of being called apart in the way of holiness, but never self-conscious as their awareness is of the God whom they worship and the people whom they serve and care for. I see such a community ardently devoted to the worship of God in a worship where awe and beauty and mystery are mingled with homeliness and fellowship. I see such a community practising fellowship among themselves as the walls of denominations yield to the discovery of unity in Christ's truth. I see such a community marked by an intellectual integrity, open both to old truth and to new discovery, a thoughtful faith which is, in St Peter's words, 'always ready to give an answer to any man who asks a reason concerning the hope that is in you.' I see such a community full of active compassion for the poor, the homeless, the hungry, the lonely. Such a community will influence the country as a whole with the ideals of service not to the group or the section but to the common good, ideals reaching far beyond our own country. Such a community will make Christ known because its members are living stones, Christ's own house in beauty and in lively steadfastness. (Ramsey, 1974, p. 86)

The second address was delivered in New Delhi, India.

The world does not hear the call to holiness, and does not care for the truth in Christ. But the world has its own care for unity, albeit conceived in a secular way; longing for peace it desires that peoples and nations shall be joined to each other and the forces which separate them removed. And the world, caring thus for unity, is shocked when the church fails to manifest it. Yet while the world's criticism might rightly humble us, we must not on that account accept the world's conception of the matter. It is not just unity, togetherness with one another, that we seek; and ecclesiastics have sometimes slipped into talking as if it were, isolating unity from the other notes of the church. It is for unity in truth and holiness that we work and pray, for that is Christ's supernatural gift to us. Let that always be made clear. A movement which concentrates on unity as an isolated concept can mislead the world and mislead us, as indeed would a movement which had the exclusive label of holiness or the exclusive label of truth. (Ramsey, 1964, p. 56)

In these two extracts we can recognise an emphasis upon unity in truth and unity in holiness, which is in fact a more profound unity than political harmony between nations and organisations. Such a unity is received as gift by those who pray and is to be incarnated by Christians in their own particular context, focused in common worship, service of the needy, intellectual openness and Christian testimony, and thereby exercising influence for the common good beyond that of the small Christian group and always operating in an international perspective.

Here we see a Christian leader firmly within the Anglican tradition as it had evolved in the modern world, going as an ambassador to regions where that tradition was developing very different manifestations.

EXERCISE
How does Ramsey's approach relate to your reading of Acts 10?

The Anglican Communion

The Anglican Communion is a worldwide family of thirty-eight self-governing member Churches or provinces, embracing more than 70 million people in 160 different countries. Anglicans thus come now from a wide range of cultures and races, and speak many different languages.

These autonomous Churches are unified through a common history, a common theology and a special relationship to the Archbishop of Canterbury.

History
The Anglican Communion developed in two main stages:
• from the seventeenth century onwards, Anglicanism spread with the political forces of colonialism to the United States of America, Australia, Canada, New Zealand and South Africa;
• from the eighteenth century, Anglicanism also spread through the work of chaplaincies and missionaries in Asia, Africa and Latin America.

Theology
The Churches of the Anglican Communion appeal to the Gospel, the apostolic Church, the Church and councils of the early centuries and the heritage of *The Book of Common Prayer* as expressing faith and order.

This was made clear in the Lambeth Quadrilateral of 1888. You will recall from chapter one that this located this theological unity in:

- the Holy Scriptures of the Old and New Testaments as containing all things necessary for salvation, and as being the rule and ultimate standard of faith;
- the Apostles' Creed and the Nicene Creed;
- Baptism and the Supper of the Lord;
- the historic episcopate, locally adapted in the methods of its administration (see Draper, 1988, pp. 5–7).

The Archbishop of Canterbury and the key Anglican forums

The Archbishop has three major roles within the Anglican Communion. One responsibility is to call together the bishops of the Anglican Communion for a major *Lambeth Conference* once every ten years. The first Lambeth Conference was held in 1867. The Archbishop also presides over the meetings of the *primates* (senior bishops in each Church) who come together every two or three years to consult on theological, social and international issues. These meetings were established in 1978. Finally, the Archbishop presides over the meetings of the *Anglican Consultative Council* which was formed at the 1968 Lambeth Conference. Every province of the Anglican Communion is represented on the Anglican Consultative Council. It has a full-time staff, plus a permanent representative at the United Nations. The work of the Council includes ecumenical dialogue, mission, communication, liturgy and social concern.

Each of these bodies provides opportunities for discussion, consultation and mutual support, but their decisions have legislative force only when a Province or a Church adopts them. The Lambeth Conference of 1930 described the Communion in the following way:

> The Anglican Communion is a fellowship, within the one Holy Catholic and Apostolic Church, of those duly constituted dioceses, provinces or regional Churches in communion with the See of Canterbury, which have the following characteristics in common:
> (a) They uphold and propagate the catholic and apostolic faith and order as they are generally set forth in *The Book of Common Prayer* as authorised in their several Churches;
> (b) They are particular or national Churches, and, as such, promote within each of their territories a national expression of Christian faith, life and worship;

(c) They are bound together not by a central legislative and executive authority, but by mutual loyalty sustained through the common council of the bishops in conference. (Lambeth Conference, 1930, p. 173)

The two issues discussed below are of particular importance for the Anglican tradition.

Dispersed authority

The Lambeth Conference of 1948 stated:

> Authority as inherited by the Anglican Communion from the undivided Church of the early centuries of the Christian era, is single in that it is derived from a single divine source, and reflects within itself the richness and historicity of the divine Revelation, the authority of the eternal Father, the incarnate Son, and the life-giving Spirit. It is distributed among Scripture, Tradition, Creeds, the ministry of the Word and Sacraments, the witness of the saints and the *consensus fidelium*, which is the continuing experience of the Holy Spirit through his faithful people in the Church. It is thus a dispersed rather than a centralised authority having many elements which combine, interact and check with each other. (Lambeth Conference, 1948, pp. 84–85)

This is the basis of unity as understood by Archbishop Ramsey. It provides a frustrating and often messy framework for discerning the mind of the Churches who constitute the Anglican Communion, not least because the process of formulating views involves:
• the commitment to wait upon God;
• acknowledging the possibility of 'further evidence';
• accepting a variety of approaches to Scripture,
• honouring contextual differences;
• involving bishops, clergy and laity in discussion, using a number of systems for debate and decision-making.

At the end of his study of the making of the worldwide Anglican Church, W M Jacob concludes:

> The Anglican Communion has studiously avoided the usual ways of maintaining unity in a communion or church, by means of a system of canon law and courts, or a single common liturgy, or a central authority. Instead unity is maintained by each church in the Communion respecting the rights of every other church. This has been

strained from time to time, but it has worked, because unity also comes from a common faith consisting of adherence to the Catholic faith as contained in the Scriptures summed up in the Apostles' Creed, as expressed in the sacraments of the Gospel and in the rites of the primitive church, and as safeguarded by the historic threefold ministry. The categories of law and compulsion are superfluous. The various parts of the Communion are held in unity as each grows in charity and in understanding of the common faith. The maintenance of unity thus is a spiritual and moral matter, not an issue of rules and law. (Jacob, 1997, p. 300)

EXERCISE

How do these comments relate to the development of Anglican tradition?

What are the problems with such a disposed approach to authority?

A national Church or an associational Church?

We may note a further key development in the form of Anglicanism as it spread throughout the world.

It is important to note that in its transplantation to North America, Anglicanism was changed from being a national communal church to an associational and gathered church. Whether in the United States, or the British colonies, it was one church amongst others; not the church of the state or the colony, and it had to compete with other churches for members, who were required to fund church buildings and the clergy. While the lay element had always been important in the Church of England, expressed through the crown and Parliament, and lay patrons, and the parish vestry, in the United States and the colonies lay people provided the financial means that enabled the Gospel to be preached, the sacraments to be administered and pastoral care to be provided. If they provided the means, they naturally wished to ensure that they would have what they considered to be a good person for the job, whether as a parish priest or as a bishop, and that they should have a voice in the governing and working of the church. This associational, congregational aspect of Anglicanism has come to pervade the

Communion, except in England, and as we have seen, it fitted and fits uncomfortably with hierarchical episcopacy, especially if it is exercised in an autocratic manner. (Jacob, 1997, p. 287)

At one level, the development of the notion of a gathered Church in the Anglican Communion beyond England could be seen to be incompatible with the parochial spirituality so central to the tradition we have been exploring. Certainly, the result has been the emergence of very different forms of Church government, with much more autonomy and greater involvement of lay Christians than has been possible in England with the roles played by Crown and Parliament.

However, at a deeper level there has been enormous congruence in terms of the Anglican tradition: its influence has been such that many gathered Churches in the Anglican Communion nevertheless subscribe to the vision of being pastorally inclusive. Yet, as the momentum of mission gathers pace in Asia and Africa, this common ground is becoming less significant. The pressures of defining an Anglican Church against other faiths is raising serious questions for this aspect of the tradition. There needs to be some vigorous dialogue and the seeking of further evidence in this area.

The evolution of the Anglican tradition, traced through the examples of Charles Gore, Josephine Butler and Henrietta Barnett, provides clues to a future ecclesiology in which local Churches may have many of the features of being associational or gathered, and yet retain their roots in the truly catholic responsibilities summarised by Michael Ramsey in his article 'What Is Anglican Theology?' (see above).

EXERCISE

📖 **Re-read the quotation from Michael Ramsey**, from his article 'What is Anglican Theology?', and state what this might imply for the modern Anglican Communion.

Personal perspectives from Anglicans worldwide

This section provides some indication of the variety of Anglicanism, as seen through the eyes of clergy and lay people in four different countries.

From Angola

I would say that the Anglican Church in Angola has its particularities which are different from other Anglican Churches. Parishes are mostly in townships where the poorer people live. In Church, choirs play a very important role. They are also strategies to attract the youth. In my parish Church, for instance, there are five choirs: two for the youth, one for the Mother's Union, one for Sunday school teachers, and an instrumental group. And all these choirs sing at every Sunday service. The songs are composed tunes in local languages, but none of the composers reads music. Furthermore, when people go to worship God, they forget the clock time. The worship is not restrained. Finally, lay people play a crucial role in the life of the Church. They are mostly given administrative responsibilities. Added to this, there are many resources and gifts from so called 'Poor Churches' that the Church in the West has denied in the past which are nowadays being valued by other members of the worldwide Anglican Communion. These in time may be the very gifts necessary for the revival of the English branch of Anglicanism. (Adao Francisco Alexandre, quoted in Redfern, 1994, pp. 168–169)

From the United States of America

My parish is one of four Episcopal congregations in the university town of Berkeley, California. Within half a mile of my church are no less than ten other Christian churches, not to mention several worship centers of other faiths. University chaplaincies of various denominations and faiths dot my street, the southern boundary of the campus. Because of the US constitutional provision of the separation of church and state, no religious organisation is allowed to locate on the property of the State-run University of California. So, although many of my congregation work, study or teach there, we are not by any means the 'University Church'.

We speak of a parish as a gathered congregation. When someone asks how big my parish is, I state that there are 225 households in our parish directory, 400 or so people on our Parish Register (Electoral Roll), 185 pledging units (covenanted givers of record) and an average Sunday attendance of just under 200. I might also speak of the annual budget, since each parish is totally self-supporting (including clergy salaries and housing) and also pays a share (or quota – in our case 20%) to support the diocese and national church organisation. We are not primarily a neighbourhood church. In fact, most of my parishioners drive by another Episcopal Church to come to St Mark's (as I do!). Especially in more urban areas, people choose their congregation more by the type of worship or programmes offered than by which church is closest. There is no system of parish boundaries.

When we undertake social ministries such as homeless programmes we normally do so in cooperation with churches of other denominations. When we want to have a voice in local government, we come as outsiders and, to have an impact we must come together (which requires a lot of coordination and negotiation!). There is no entrée into state schools. Despite the fact that a much larger percentage of the population attends church regularly in the US than in the UK, religion is not woven into the fabric of governance and no one religious group can claim the kind of majority membership (albeit largely nominal) of the Church of England. We Episcopalians are not even one percent of the population. (The Revd C Robbins Clark, personal communication)

From Uganda

The coming of the missionaries of the Church Missionary Society (CMS) from England in 1877 marked the beginning for the Anglican Church in Uganda. On the whole, amidst conflict and persecution, the Anglican Church of Uganda continues to experience a high rate of growth. Christianity in Uganda has demonstrated its power in many ways; for example in successful evangelism where the laity are in the forefront reaching out to others in their families, in places of work, shops, streets, factories, schools, on buses/trains and soon everyone is eager to be involved in sharing the good news about Jesus Christ. Christians in Uganda are not afraid to speak up about their faith with whoever they come across. In other words, faith to them is never a private affair. They usually tell others of what the Lord has done in their lives and encourage them to have the same experience. Certainly, they are quite sure of and genuinely 'proud' of their faith. In Britain however, the reverse is evident. People are not open about their faith. A lot of people do not want to be too involved with church matters. An hour for a Sunday Service is all they can afford to give. Time is far too precious to be wasted on 'religious' things. What is disheartening is that some clergy are not inclined to engage in the active spreading of the Gospel. They are more comfortable in positions of pastoral ministry as opposed to involvement in something pro-active. In view of this I think there are lessons to be learnt by Christians in England from the church abroad.

Many of the Anglican churches in Uganda function primarily with lay leadership. This, I believe is among the things English Anglicanism needs to learn from other parts of the Anglican Communion. My experience of English Anglicanism is that there are multi-church parishes, some of which have only monthly services. I suppose if the laity were deployed they could keep all churches open every Sunday. It is important that both the Christian laity and clergy unite in their dynamic witness.

In Uganda, like anywhere else in the Anglican Communion, worship is vital. Ugandan Christians worship God with their whole being. They clap hands, dance, use local musical instruments and encourage spontaneity. On the contrary, worship in English Anglicanism lacks joy. It is so 'serious' and glum. No doubt a lot of young people do not find church exciting at all. So they decide to keep their feet out of it all. English Anglicanism therefore needs to learn to make worship lively and more appealing to young people. The Church should try to avoid the tendency of a 'one-man-show' in worship. Worship should be inclusive.

The Anglican Church in Uganda takes spirituality very seriously. The influence of elements of the revival is still evident in church today. Personal testimony, or witness and fellowship are emphasised. In England people tend to take everything for granted and do not spend so much time in prayer (for provision of daily needs), whilst in Uganda there is a greater dependence on God to provide and protect. Ugandan Christians always pray before a journey, for example, a Christian in England just hops in the car and drives off.

In addition, emphasis is put on Bible study. This enhances a personal knowledge of the word of God as well as fostering communal life. Certainly family life is elevated. It is noteworthy that Christians do not place a dichotomy between proclamation of the Gospel and social transformation. In other words, Christians live the Gospel. Interestingly, a lot of Christians in England have little expectation that God will act so they feel they have to do it themselves as individuals. This has caused a lot of isolation instead of God's children living as the family of God.

Having said this, it is important for me to note that there is a lot that the Anglican Church in Uganda needs to learn from English Anglicanism too. (Beatrice N Musindi, quoted in Redfern, 1994, pp. 169–170)

From Korea

Anglican mission has to be a dialogue between the Old Anglicanism and other active subjects in other cultures. If we can say anything about the failure and success of mission, it is dependent upon this dialogue. The true dialogue will be the background for the new understanding of Anglicanism.

The demand for this true dialogue asks us to change the basic pattern of Anglican study. Until now, the study of Anglicanism has been about the Old Anglicanism which means a peculiar English religious experience. And the understanding of this Old Anglicanism has been regarded as the most important key to explaining the present situation of Anglican Churches in other continents. In other words, those terms like 'High Church' and 'Low Church' traditions, 'evangelism' and 'Oxford movements', 'USPG' and 'CMS', have been used as crucial tools of explanation. But this is only a monologue. In fact, the Anglican mission as monologue has been too successful!

But the true dialogue has been made in the most intimate contact with the questions and prayers of people. In this dialogue, as I see it, an idealistic apologetic for Anglicanism loses its power. Rather, such a dialogue will have the effect of shaking the foundations of the old Anglicanism. And for new Churches, it will be the experience of new birth. But the true dialogue has yet to take concrete form in the Anglican Communion. Usually it is only experienced in 'abnormal' processes like the conflicts within dioceses or provinces, when the necessity of a new understanding of Anglicanism has been raised. However, at a local level, dialogue is often happening invisibly as numerous questions are being raised everyday.

Fundamentally, the answers to these questions are not given by the explanation that Anglicanism is different from Protestantism and Roman-Catholicism. The questions which I am raising are more fundamental than the question of a denominational identity. Rather, these questions are about the authenticity of Anglican mission in a given context. Therefore, these questions require us Anglicans to stand face to face with our God in the context where we find ourselves, as I believe, here is the place where the discussion about Anglicanism can overcome the English or British boundary. Therefore, the first task for the new understanding of our Communion is not in praising English Anglican history but in collecting and clarifying those questions which have been raised acutely in all places within Anglican Communion. (The Revd Yang Guen-Seok, quoted in Redfern, 1994, pp. 163–174)

> **EXERCISE**
> What are the implications of these different reflections for the Anglican tradition?
>
> Can you discern directions for future development?
>
> What could your local church learn from these remarks?

The Lambeth Conference 1998

I was privileged to attend this conference and to meet people from every part of the Anglican Communion. At one level there were signs of the tensions we have discerned within the Communion, most especially in relation to:

- the use of Scripture;
- human sexuality and the valuing of experience;
- theological frameworks and methodologies;
- attitudes to authority;
- processes for decision-making;
- parochial or associational ecclesiologies;
- the place of women.

Of course, these issues are all major areas for discussion and dispute in the wider world beyond the Church, so we should not be surprised that they featured so strongly. And yet, in terms of the Anglican tradition the most powerful elements of the Conference were:

- common worship, using a variety of resources yet each bearing a clear family resemblance;
- a common commitment to the marks of the Lambeth Quadrilateral (Scripture, creeds, sacraments, episcopacy);
- a common approach to the theological enterprise, with exploration, the comparing of independent testimonies, recognition of the importance of a distinctive 'mould' for our times, and an openness to 'further evidence'.

The passion, the graciousness, the focus on prayer and the willingness to offer public response, while recognising the inevitable elements of incompleteness and provisionality, bore all the hallmarks of fundamentalisms in dialogue, and provided an important example to all the various branches and levels of the Anglican Communion as similar issues of human need and frailty are confronted by the Gospel committed to us.

EXERCISE

What are the five most important characteristics of the Anglican tradition for today? How do these relate to the marks of Anglicanism mentioned in chapter one?

How might being Anglican provide resources for connecting different cultures?

'Anglicanism exists in the eye of the believer.' Do you agree?

📖 **Read Acts 11.** Can you discern any resonances with the Anglican tradition? You might like to consider:
  - dispute between those guided by Scripture and tradition, and those discerning 'further evidence';
  - decision-making after discussion and debate;
  - appeal to the words of Jesus and to the manifestation of the Holy Spirit;
  - all sides joined in praising God in common worship;
  - the wider outreach still depended upon repentance: there was no easy accommodation of other cultures;
  - differences were brought together by God's gift: to which the Church responds;
  - the Gospel was taken to other places;
  - in different places there were different responses (in Antioch they were called Christians);
  - there was a strong sense of these different Churches being in communion with each other. This was rooted in:
    a. a common Gospel – the Good News about the Lord Jesus;
    b. apostles who co-operated across the different communities;
    c. a common system of local elders as Church leaders;
    d. a commitment to mutual support.

Further reading

Avis, P (1989), *Anglicanism and the Christian Church*, Edinburgh, T and T Clark.

Bunting, I (ed.) (1996), *Celebrating the Anglican Way*, London, Hodder and Stoughton.

Chadwick, O (1990), *Michael Ramsey: a life*, Oxford, Oxford University Press.

Hannaford, R (ed.) (1996), *The Future of Anglicanism*, Leominster, Gracewing.

Jacob, W M (1997), *The Making of the Anglican Church Worldwide*, London, SPCK.

McGrath, A (1993), *The Renewal of Anglicanism*, London, SPCK.

Ramsey, M (1964), *Canterbury Essays and Addresses*, London, SPCK.

Ramsey, M (1974), *Canterbury Pilgrim*, London, SPCK.

Sachs, W L (1993), *The Transformation of Anglicanism*, Cambridge, Cambridge University Press.

Sykes, S (1995), *Unashamed Anglicanism*, London, Darton, Longman and Todd.

REFERENCES

Barnett, H (1918), *Canon Barnett*, London, John Murray.

Barnett, H (1930), *Matters that Matter*, London, John Murray.

Barnett, S A and H (1894), *Essays on Social Reform*, London, Longmans, Green.

Bartlett, T (1839), *Memoirs of Joseph Butler*, London, J W Parker.

Bernard, J H (1900), *The Works of Bishop Butler*, London, Macmillan.

Bourne, E C E (1947), *The Anglicanism of William Laud*, London, SPCK.

Butler, A S G (1954), *Portrait of Josephine Butler*, London, Faber and Faber.

Butler, J (1892), *Recollections of George Butler*, Bristol, Arrowsmith.

Butler, J (1897), *The Analogy of Religion*, ed. W E Gladstone, Oxford, Clarendon.

Chadwick, O (1990), *Michael Ramsey: a life*, Oxford, Oxford University Press.

Cunliffe, C (ed.) (1992), *Joseph Butler's Moral and Religious Thought*, Oxford, Clarendon.

Davies, H (1975), *Worship and Theology in England*, Vol. II, Princeton, New Jersey, Princeton University Press.

Draper, J (ed.) (1988), *Communion and Episcopacy*, Oxford, Ripon College Cuddesdon.

General Synod of the Church of England (1992), *Report of Proceedings*, 23, 3, London, Church House Publishing.

Gore, C (1891), *The Incarnation of the Son of God*, London, John Murray.

Gore, C (1892), *The Social Doctrine of the Sermon on the Mount*, London, Percival.

Gore, C (1898), *St Paul's Epistle to the Ephesians*, London, John Murray.

Gore, C (1905), *Roman Catholic Claims*, London, Longmans, Green.

Gore, C (1909), *Orders and Unity*, London, John Murray.

Gore, C (1930), *The Philosophy of the Good Life*, London, John Murray.

Herbert, G (1956), *The Country Parson and Selected Poems*, London, SCM.

Hooker, R (1907), *Of the Laws of Ecclesiastical Polity* (Everyman's Library), London, Dent.

Inge, W R (1905), *Studies in the English Mystics*, London, Longmans, Green.

Jacob, W M (1997), *The Making of the Anglican Church Worldwide*, London, SPCK.

Johnson, G W and L A (eds) (1909), *Josephine E Butler: an autobiographical memoir*, London, Arrowsmith.

Lambeth Conference (1930), *Encyclical Letter from the Bishops together with the Resolutions and Reports*, London, SPCK.

Lambeth Conference (1948), *Encyclical Letter from the Bishops together with the Resolutions and Reports,* London, SPCK.

Lambeth Conference (1968), *Encyclical Letter from the Bishops together with the Resolutions and Reports,* London, SPCK.

Laud, W (1847–1860), *Works,* eds W Scott and J Bliss, Library of Anglo-Catholic Theology, Oxford, J H Parker, seven volumes.

Law, W (1978), *A Serious Call To A Devout and Holy Life,* New York, Paulist Press.

Marshall, M (1984), *The Anglican Church Today and Tomorrow,* Oxford, Mowbray.

Maurice, F (1885), *The Life of F D Maurice,* London, Macmillan.

Ramsey, M (1945), What is Anglican Theology? *Theology,* 48, 2–6.

Ramsey, M (1964), *Canterbury Essays and Addresses,* London, SPCK.

Ramsey, M (1974), *Canterbury Pilgrim,* London, SPCK.

Reardon, B M G (1971), *Religious Thought in the Victorian Age,* London, Longman.

Redfern, A L J (1994), *The Anglican Tradition,* Birmingham, Aston Training Scheme.

Stephenson, A M G (1978), *Anglicanism and the Lambeth Conferences,* London, SPCK.

Stranks, C J (1961), *Anglican Devotion,* London, SCM.

Walton, I (1973), *The Lives of John Donne, Richard Hooker, George Herbert, Henry Wotton and Robert Sanderson,* with an introduction by G Saintsbury, London, Oxford University Press.

GLOSSARY AND BIOGRAPHY

Alternative Service Book a new book of common prayer produced by the Church of England in 1980. The 1662 version remains normative.

Aquinas, Thomas (c. 1225–1274) a philosopher and theologian who was declared a 'Doctor of the Church' by the Roman Catholic Church in 1567.

Aristotle (384–322 BC) a Greek philosopher who had a great influence upon St Thomas Aquinas and who has provided a basis for western philosophical theology since the middle ages.

Barnett, Henrietta (1851–1936) wife of Canon Samuel Barnett, vicar of St Jude's Whitechapel from 1873 to 1894. Together they established Toynbee Hall and schemes for religious and cultural improvements in the East End of London. They produced books of essays on 'practicable socialism'.

Book of Common Prayer the official service book of the Church of England, authorised by the Act of Uniformity in 1662.

Butler, Joseph (1692–1752) Bishop of Bristol (1738) and Durham (1750). One of the greatest teachers of natural theology and ethics in the Church of England since the Reformation. His works were widely read in the nineteenth century and were acknowledged as influential by Newman.

Butler, Josephine (1826–1906) Anglican social reformer, particularly concerned with the issue of prostitution, both in England and on the Continent. Also a noted teacher of spirituality.

Caroline divines a school of Anglican theological teachers of the seventeenth century.

Chantry an organisation that provided prayers for the souls of the departed and also offered resources for pastoral care and education.

Convocation an assembly of the clergy of the Church of England.

Fathers of the Church theological teachers of the age immediately succeeding the New Testament period, who are often seen as being authoritative in matters of doctrine.

Gore, Charles (1853–1932) Bishop of Worcester (1902), Birmingham (1905) and Oxford (1911–1919). Founder of the Community of the Resurrection (1892), co-founder of the Christian Social Union (1889). Prolific author and popular teacher.

Herbert, George (1593–1633) poet and priest. His most famous prose work, *A Priest to the Temple: or the Country Parson*, is a classic description of the ideal country parson. Some of his poems have become well-known hymns.

Hobbes, Thomas (1588–1679) philosopher who challenged the idea of the divine right of kings, by arguing that sovereignty is ultimately derived from the people and held by the monarch by contract. His theory of human conduct was based upon natural science rather than traditional theology.

Hooker, Richard (c. 1554–1600) Anglican divine whose *Treatise on the Laws of Ecclesiastical Polity* provided a theological rationale for the Church of England that was distinct from both puritanism and Roman Catholicism.

Lambeth Conference ten-yearly meeting of the bishops of the Anglican Communion.

Laud, William (1573–1648) Archbishop of Canterbury (1633–1645), adviser of Charles I. Executed by order of Parliament. Upheld the divine right of kings. Broad and conciliatory in matter of doctrine, but rigorous with regard to Church order.

Law, William (1686–1761) a spiritual writer who had great influence on John Wesley (Methodism and the Evangelical Revival) and J H Newman (the Oxford Movement).

Maurice, Frederick Denison (1805–1872) Anglican theologian, educator and Christian socialist.

Minor Orders a range of ministerial functions assistant to the major orders of bishop, priest and deacon.

More, Hannah (1745–1833) a religious writer who established schools and friendly societies, and encouraged movements for adult learning and poor relief.

Newman, John Henry (1801–1890) a leading figure in the catholic revival in the Church of England, who became a Roman Catholic in 1845 and was made a cardinal in 1879. Influential through his preaching, his teaching about spirituality, his ideas about the development of Christian doctrine and his *Idea of a University*.

Ramsey, Michael (1904–1988) Archbishop of Canterbury (1961–1974), influential as a Christian teacher and apologist. He was prominent in his oversight of the Anglican Communion and as a theologian.

Simeon, Charles (1759–1863) incumbent of Holy Trinity Church, Cambridge for fifty-three years and a fellow of King's College, Cambridge. He was an important leader of the Evangelical Revival in the Church of England, particularly through training of clergy, establishing overseas missions and organising Church patronage to support evangelical principles.

Synodical Government the 'General Synod' is the formal meeting of bishops, clergy and laity for the government of the Church of England. It was established in its present form in 1969.

Thirty-Nine Articles the doctrinal statements of the Church of England, attached to *The Book of Common Prayer*.

Vatican Council a gathering of Roman Catholic Bishops, first summoned in 1869 by Pope Pius IX. The Second Vatican Council met from 1962 to 1965.

Wesley, John (1703–1791) his pioneering missionary work in the Church of England led to the foundation of the Methodist Movement. An outstanding Christian leader and teacher whose work stimulated widespread revival in eighteenth-century England.

INDEX OF THEMES

Applying for the Church Colleges' Certificate Programme

The certificate programme is available in Anglican Church Colleges of Higher Education throughout England and Wales. There are currently hundreds of students on this programme, many with no previous experience of study of this kind. There are no entry requirements. Some people choose to take Certificate courses for their own interest and personal growth, others take these courses as part of their training for ministry in the church. Some go on to complete the optional assignments and, after the successful completion of three courses, gain the Certificate. Courses available through the *Exploring Faith: theology for life* series are ideal for establishing ability and potential for studying theology and biblical studies at degree level, and they provide credit onto degree programmes.

For further details of the Church Colleges' Certificate programme, related to this series, please contact the person responsible for Adult Education in your local diocese or one of the colleges at the addresses provided:

The Administrator of Part-time Programmes, Department of Theology and Religious Studies, Chester College, Parkgate Road, CHESTER, CH1 4BJ ☎ 01244 375444

The Registry, Roehampton Institute, Froebel College, Roehampton Lane, LONDON, SW15 5PJ ☎ 020 8392 3087

The Registry, Canterbury Christ Church University College, North Holmes Road, CANTERBURY, CT1 1QU ☎ 01227 767700

The Registry, College of St Mark and St John, Derriford Road, PLYMOUTH, PL6 8BH ☎ 01752 636892

The Registry, Trinity College, CARMARTHEN, Carmarthenshire, SA31 3EP ☎ 01267 676767

Church Colleges' Programme, The Registry, King Alfred's College, Sparkford Road, WINCHESTER, SO22 4NR ☎ 01962 841515

Part-time Programmes, The Registry, College of St Martin, Bowerham Road, LANCASTER, LA1 3JD ☎ 01524 384529